I0826529

CHAPTER XII

The joy of the reward.. 159

Last words.. 167

The Faith I Never Lost

Follow your Inner Voice

Adriana Tapia

The information provided in this book is solely intended to share life experiences, the author's factual perspective, and does not have the purpose of pointing out or holding any person or institution responsible. The author and the publicist are not responsible for any diagnosis, treatment or act carried out by any person who has read this book, or has listened to it by third parties, since any decision made related to such acts and its consequences will be the sole responsibility of whoever carries them out.

INDEX

DEDICATION... 9

INTRODUCTION... 11

ACKNOWLEDGMENTS... 13

CHAPTER I

Everything starts with a huge desire.................... 15

CHAPTER II

Searching for my dream to come true.................. 25

Life gives you surprises... 32

CHAPTER III

When reality exceeds the unimaginable.............. 39

CIIAPTER IV

Love overcomes pain... 45

We never know the path we will have to travel..... 51

CHAPTER V

A grand change in my life................................. 61

When challenges shape our character.................... 63

CHAPTER VI

The frantic search for solutions............................ 75

CHAPTER VII

The right path... 87

Always listen to your inner voice.......................... 92

CHAPTER VIII

Acceptance and adaptation............................... 103

CHAPTER IX

When two dreams come together........................ 111

Do whatever it takes. 125

CHAPTER X

The blessings begin.. 127

Another dream comes true................................ 131

CHAPTER XI

The impossible is possible................................ 139

Another dream, another blessing....................... 153

CHAPTER XII

The joy of the reward.. 159

Last words.. 167

Dedicated to:

I dedicate this book first to my children, Caroline and Matthew, whom I love with all my heart and have been my strongest yearning and the reason of so much effort to finally achieve having them with me; they were my most sublime dream, whom I loved even before conceiving them.

To my husband, Brian, with whom I have lived all this experience of being parents at all costs and who supported me in the dream of writing this book.

Introduction

In this book I share the story that my husband and I lived, with Caroline our first child. It is a story of love, of faith, of hope, but also of so much pain and effort as well as learning experiences.

Through more than six years of Caroline's struggle for life, I learned to strengthen and hold on to my faith, my intuition, the perseverance and visualization of a healthy and happy daughter.

It is the story of the process of giving birth to a premature baby, saving her life and nurturing her to the normal development of all her physical functions, during which I had to overcome desperation, suffering, pain. By God's grace this brought out my greatest strength and the best side of myself.

You may be going through a similar situation right now, such as an illness with one of your children, or you may be going through a different kind of tough time in your life. You need to strengthen yourself through faith to go beyond that stage, which sometimes seems endless when we see nothing but what we are experiencing at that moment.

My intention is to help you with my story and inspire you, so you can get past yours.

I will tell you step by step what I went through for over six years, the anguish and suffering of watching time go by without finding out if or how my daughter could survive, waiting and wishing that she had a normal life. This was my major hope from day to day.

Acknowledgments

I thank the Lord for giving me the strength and guidance to find the right way to achieve the greatest wish of my life. Also I want to thank my parents, Rosa Martha and Marco Antonio, who supported me by taking care of my daughter when I could not take care of her.

Thanks to my in-laws, Robert and Marsha, especially my mother-in-law who now rests in peace. While she lived she always helped us in every way possible. She lived in Alabama, and recently had recovered from cancer surgery, but she still traveled to help out with our children. I am also grateful that she was one of the few people who always recognized my efforts and tenacity to help my daughter.

Thanks to my younger sister, Elizabeth, for her unconditional support by receiving me at her home for almost a month. She always cared for me and the most valuable thing she gave me was her constant companionship at my side with her hospital visits and her presence at Matthew's birth. Also thanks to her for helping me with her valuable ideas for writing this book.

Thanks to my sister, Rosa Martha, who without thinking twice, donated her blood to Caroline when it was necessary. I also thank Mrs. Jovita, my mother's assistant at her home for more than ten years; she cared enough to whip up new recipes for Caroline so she could eat them.

Thanks to my husband's uncle and aunt, Tom and Debbie, who helped us when we needed it the most.

To the doctors who cared for my daughter since she was born and those who diagnosed her correctly, thank you to each and every person who helped me or helped my daughter to continue developing.

Thank you all very much!!!

CHAPTER I

Everything starts with a huge desire

I believe that the strongest and most powerful love that a woman can experience is the love for her children. Even though they are a great responsibility and sometimes we become a little crazy, exhausted in the daily job of taking care and educating them, I, like many other women in the world, had an enormous desire to be a mother. It was one of my greatest dreams and longings in my heart.

I am from the city of Tijuana, a city in northwestern Mexico that borders the state of California in the United States. It is very common for people who live on either side of the border, to cross from one country to another to do many different daily activities, such as: visiting their family, going shopping, enjoying entertainment, keeping medical appointments, etc. There is even a personnel exchange in companies called expatriate jobs, given the territorial proximity that exists.

This is how I met my husband, Brian, who is originally from Alabama. For employment reasons he had been living and working in my city for a few months in a U.S. company. A friend who was working in the same company as my husband introduced us, and from that day on we started dating and getting to know each other.

Shortly after that first date, we began going out steady, though there was some difficulty communicating, due to language issues. Ironically, English had never been my strong suit; however, when strong ties are created, obstacles are gradually removed.

We developed a beautiful relationship, as we got to know each other little by little. We traveled, which enabled us to enjoy each other in various settings. The love that was born between us was a sufficient force to break the language barriers. Over time I learned to speak and understand English more and Brian studied Spanish, although the language with which we both communicate has always been English. Even today I admit that I have not mastered the language 100%, especially for work or in deeper issues such as medical.

After four and a half years of dating, we married at 33 years of age and decided to continue living in the city of Tijuana.

Brian and I planned to let another year pass before having our first child, so after that time, when I was 34 years old, we decided that we were ready to have our first child. I was not a young girl but neither was I over-aged. Doctors always recommend having children before the age of 35, which is why I decided to seek medical assistance to get pregnant after a few months of trying with no success. I didn't want to waste any more time trying to conceive my first child.

We both had health insurance, including doctor and hospital care in the United States, since the company was North American.

I started going to the gynecologist, because I wanted to be as healthy as possible to get pregnant. The doctor sent me to complete some exams and lab studies, including an ultrasound, which showed that I had a problem in the womb.

The diagnosis was **uterus septum**, and the doctor explained that this anomaly was congenital. It consists of the uterus being divided into two cavities that are separated by a kind of partition formed by a fibrous or muscular wall. This wall can divide only part of the uterus (partial uterus septum) or completely divide it (complete uterus septum). The uterus septum or septate uterus is the most common congenital anomaly of the uterus. It occurs during the formation of the woman's uterus in the mother's womb.

This malformation is a risk factor for recurrent miscarriage, but it does not always prevent pregnancy. One of the most common problems is that the cavities are too small for the embryo to develop, or that the placenta is implanted in a wall with insufficient supply of nutrients. Even a small septum or uterine septum reduces the chances of pregnancy.

For me this diagnosis was a great surprise since I had previously done some ultrasounds and this malformation in my womb had not been detected. In addition, women in my family had never been in this situation or experienced any problem conceiving during their pregnancies or deliveries. The doctor who was treating me at the time did not attribute much importance to this anatomical problem. He told me that most likely when consulting a fertility doctor, he would want me to undergo a corrective operation, which in his opinion was not necessary.

However, I was not satisfied, and I did not listen to his recommendation. I followed my intuition and went to a specialized clinic to see a fertility specialist.

Thank God we had health insurance, which covered all the expenses generated by the exams, tests and studies required. How important it is to have this backing. Insurance is the best investment that can be made, since it gives peace of mind economically when facing a health situation of any kind, which can occur to anyone and at the least expected time. In addition to the economic aspect, it is the security that your sick loved one will be cared for and treated with whatever it takes to regain their health. We don't typically think about this when we are healthy, but there can always be surprising emergency situations, and more so when our children's pregnancies and births are involved. Believe me, it is a huge emotional relief, especially when those we love the most need specialized attention to be able to live.

I had the studies and tests done on me at the fertility clinic to assign me a treatment and correct the womb situation. However, several days later I realized that I was pregnant!

It was a moment of emotional shock. On one hand I was very happy, but on the other hand I was very worried. First, because of the risk of abortion due to the malformation that had been detected in the uterus; second, because in order to make sure that there was nothing physical that would interfere with conception, they would have to perform a clinical study called **hysterosalpingography**, which is a radiological technique used to detect infertility problems. The uterine cavity and the fallopian tubes are explored, introducing a drug that can cause malformations in babies.

The only resource left for me to do was prayer. I prayed with all my strength and with all my faith, asking God that my baby would not be affected by this study, and that she could grow and develop as a completely healthy fetus.

The other action I took immediately was to put myself in the hands of the gynecologist to review and care for my pregnancy. Yet, within a few weeks what I feared so much occurred, an unforced miscarriage causing the loss of my first conceived baby.

I underwent the practice of curettage, feeling great sadness to think that I could have the remains of a lifeless baby inside of me, although I was only a few weeks pregnant. I remember leaving the hospital quite in shock by all of this, and I couldn't seem to stop crying. I was dealing with a sickening loss, in addition to the feeling of guilt I felt for having this study be carried out, because I thought that perhaps this had caused the abortion, although the doctors explained that these cases happen naturally and not because of something the mother did or did not do.

I knew that it is common and natural for women who lose their babies like this to have that feeling of real loss; but living it and feeling it in my own experience, I can say that it is one of the deeper pains that a mother can experience. My husband's reaction to this event was quiet and to some extent I felt that he considered my grief somewhat exaggerated. But I was truly overwhelmed.

A few weeks later I began to feel calmer and less guilty, reflecting on the fact that I had not caused the death of the baby. I started letting my faith sooth my pain by accepting that everything happens for a reason and that God's plan is always good, I began to see things with more hope, I had to move on with my life and focus on improving my physical condition. I had the possibility to correct the abnormality of the uterus through surgery and be able to get pregnant again with the assurance of having a normal pregnancy and giving birth to a healthy baby with no complications. Believing that God wanted it like this for a reason gave me peace of mind and confidence that everything in the future would be fine.

According to statistical information from the Mayo Clinic site, it is estimated that between 10 and 20% of pregnancies result in a miscarriage before 20 weeks of gestation, and the rate is believed to be even higher, since there are occasions in which some women do not even realize or report that there was a pregnancy.

It took more than six months from the curettage treatment to have the operation, and during that time I sought to return to my daily life. At times I felt desperate. I wanted time to go by quickly, to have the surgery, and be able to get pregnant again. At times I saw the loss of the baby as a delay to my plans. I felt the pressure of time because of my age, but it would be several more months before I was able to have the operation and then a few more to have an opportunity to conceive.

This is when I learned that many times, even if we have a plan, life has different ones for us, and we can't control everything around us. Little by little I realized that there are detours that occur in life and we have to wait for the right moment. Despite what happened, I was not afraid to seek another pregnancy, at least not in those moments. On the contrary, I was yearning to be able to try again.

Finally in March 2008 an operation called **Hysteroscopy Metroplasty** was carried out, which consists of removing a wall that divides the uterus into two parts and makes it look heart-shaped. This frees the uterus cavity and provides the baby enough space to grow. It was an outpatient surgery with general anesthesia, non-invasive. Thanks to the technology nowadays they only made two small incisions which left virtually no scars.

When I woke up from the operation I was not in pain; the only discomfort I had was nausea and dizziness, which personally I get after anesthesia. After a few hours at home, I started to feel a severe pain that fortunately was controlled with medication. The inconvenience lasted for the next five days, but by the next week I was able to start my normal activities.

"Desire backed by faith knows no such word as impossible" -Napoleon Hill

The surgeon's report was that the uterus had been successfully corrected; it had been left in optimal conditions to carry a normal pregnancy.

CHAPTER II

Searching for my dream to come true

Hope is the certainty that something makes sense, regardless of how it turns out.

After about three months of recovery from surgery, the doctor gave me an oral treatment for three months to assist ovulation. During that time, my husband and I traveled to the city of Boston to the baptism of my twin nephews, Diego and Mateo, sons of my sister, Elizabeth, who lived there at the time. After breakfast at the baptism party, suddenly and for no apparent reason I began to feel a general discomfort and nausea. I was thankful that symptoms were not repeated. But that's when we suspected that I could be pregnant.

We took the opportunity to walk around and get to know the city for a few days. My husband returned home and I decided to stay for a couple of days with my sister to help her with her twins.

On one of those days, we had to take one of the babies to the Children's Hospital for a medical checkup. I accompanied my sister, but I stayed away from the radiology and X-ray area, I knew in the back of my mind there was a chance that I was pregnant and, thinking that I could put my baby at risk, I didn't want to get near that particular area. I didn't say anything to my sister because I wanted to be sure first with a pregnancy test. My husband and I had also agreed not to say anything to anybody until I was a few months into my pregnancy.

A few days later, still in my sister's house, I took the home pregnancy test, getting the long-awaited "**positive**" result; I couldn't bear the excitement and phoned my husband to give him the wonderful news!

Once the fertility doctor was sure of the pregnancy, having done the blood tests twice to see the hormone count, positively corroborating the news. I was discharged and sent to the gynecologist in order to continue routine checkups during the pregnancy process that looked to be normal. I felt very confident and calm that everything was happening perfectly. My husband and I were more than happy, super excited to tell the news to the whole family and share with them our enormous joy but we chose not to say anything till the first quarter of pregnancy was fulfilled. Because of the previous painful experience, we feared that something similar could happen and we did not want to give false expectations to the family and make them go through that again.

During those first three months, I felt some anxiety and started experiencing negative thoughts. Suddenly I was afraid, doubting whether this time my baby would be born at full pregnancy. I sought to redirect my thoughts, focus my mind to think positively, and visualize that this time it would be successful. I put all my trust in God and the doctor who cared for me, because I felt that I had been properly cared for.

At the beginning of the second trimester, my gynecologist sent me to a specialist to check if there were any abnormalities in my baby, since I was already 35 years old. I do not know if all gynecologists do this type of check-up, but mine did. While attending my appointment with the specialist, I remember that he began to explain to me all the variety of possible abnormalities that my baby could have because of my age; however, just listening to the conversation made me automatically reject any test and left the doctor's office. It made no sense to me to think about abnormalities much less look for them. They wanted to perform the amniocentesis test, which consists of inserting a fine needle into the uterus through the abdomen, to extract a small sample of the amniotic fluid that surrounds the fetus and analyze it. I had read that this test can cause abortions in 1% of the cases, so I decided not to do this study and above all I preferred to have confidence in God that my baby would arrive fine in to this world.

Every day my desire to be a mother increased. I longed to be able to carry my baby in my arms. So at approximately fourteen weeks of pregnancy I did an ultrasound study in Tijuana. We wanted to know the sex of the baby, and the study showed that it was a girl and that her development looked very good. We decided to do the ultrasound in Tijuana, since doctors in the United States wait until approximately four months of gestation to inform the patient if it will be a boy or a girl. These are some advantages of living in a border area, having access to different services depending on the patient's wishes.

We received the news with great joy. I will never forget the beautiful experience when I listened to the heartbeat of my baby and watched her move around like a miniature. It was an impressive thing to see that there was life inside of me. I can't even explain what I felt in words; I had tears of happiness knowing that everything was going very well and that the little being would soon be in my arms.

So we decided to make the happy announcement to our family, and we chose Thanksgiving day. We prepared a rich dinner. My husband had also made a beautiful video with the ultrasound we had recorded. We just told them that we wanted to share a video with them, and we started to see it on TV. They all congratulated us and they were very happy for us, with lots of hugs and wishes for happiness with this beautiful baby who was on the way.

This custom of meeting around Thanksgiving was not one of my own family's traditions, and although many Tijuana residents have adopted it, we have not. My parents are originally from inland states of Mexico, far from the American cultural influence. But since I got married, and Brian and I started celebrating it at home with my whole family, this became a new tradition which we celebrate every year.

The event was very special and exciting for both families. It was the first grandchild from my husband's side and there were already several boys in my family, so it would be the first girl in the whole family! Not only did we expect one more member of the family with great joy, but there was a special touch with her arrival for all!

For the 2008 Christmas holidays we even traveled to Birmingham, Alabama to my in-law's home with my husband's whole family. My mother-in-law was so happy because she would finally become a grandmother. She bought countless things for our baby, and even helped us choose and buy the furniture for her room.

We were all very excited and happy with the arrival of our princess, my husband painted the room assigned for her in shades of green and pastel pink--colors that we had chosen after seeing specialized decorative magazines. We started the preparations for the baby shower, working on the invitations, looking for the right room for the event, choosing the decoration, etc., all preparations for the traditional welcome party to the new family member.

Just as many first-time mothers, I bought myself a book to guide me in the evolution of pregnancy week after week, to study and inform myself of the entire development of my baby. I wanted to know all the changes and symptoms that might happen in my body in order to be alert and take care of me as much as possible.

However, approximately between the 24th and 25th weeks of my pregnancy I began to feel something strange, like a mixture of colic similar to symptoms that cause menstruation and very intense kicks of the baby along with a feeling of contractions and stretches within the womb. I mention sensation because at those times I did not know exactly how a contraction felt--it was a new feeling I'd never had before.

I did not pay undue attention to these symptoms. I continued to guide myself week by week from the pregnancy book I was reading, and the authors referred to the fact that it was normal after week 20 to start feeling the so-called contractions of Braxton Hicks, those pre-training exercises that the uterus does before delivery. I assumed that these discomforts were normal, and I chose not to notify the doctor of any of this.

The following days I remember perfectly. It was on a weekend, I was lying on the couch in my home watching television when I started to feel stronger kicks. Although I felt some discomfort, there was very little pain. Even on that day, I didn't give it a second thought.

After having lived through what would follow from that moment, my advice to any pregnant woman, and especially to new mothers, is to notify your doctors of any symptoms you have. It is better to ask too much. Don't be shy about it because you want by all means to prevent any anomaly. After my experience, I would recommend reading a pregnancy book, if you want to understand a little bit more on how your body is changing and what is happening inside of you, but never to guide you in what you are really feeling, never to replace the checkups and opinions of the specialist. In the same way I consider that it is very important to always search until you find a doctor who will take care of you and be patient with you to clear all your doubts and questions.

Sometimes when we have health insurance where we have to limit ourselves to choosing a doctor from a list, it takes us some time to find the right doctor for each person, but it is extremely important and also very useful to give yourself time to research various opinions from people on the Internet who have already been treated by that specific doctor, as well as finding out about the medical experience they have.

Life gives you surprises

The following Monday, I woke up with some bleeding. It was at that moment when I realized that something was wrong and decided to go to the hospital. My mom lived next to my house so I asked her to please take me to the hospital in San Diego. Once crossing the border, it would take us about 25 minutes to get there. I preferred to tell my mom to bring me to the hospital instead of waiting more time for my husband to arrive. The doctors treating me were waiting for me, and my mom was very worried--I think even more than me. Up to this point I did not realize the seriousness of the situation. I thought that perhaps they would recommend rest and nothing else.

I arrived at the hospital very calm. I didn't feel sick, nor did I feel any pain. However after the doctor's did the initial checkup, he told me that I had ruptured membranes, and that I could no longer go home. They would have to move me in an ambulance to the hospital specializing in preterm births, where I would remain in bed as it was necessary to be under absolute and strict rest. If I didn't do so, the baby could be born at any time, four months earlier than expected. Now that I see how the events were occurring, it was a blessing to have been so close to an institution with this type of experience.

It was only after listening to the doctor that I realized how delicate the situation was. It had a huge emotional impact to learn what was happening so when the doctor left the room I just began to cry and feel very afraid of losing my baby. My pregnancy was advanced, but not enough to be able to guarantee keeping her alive or completely healthy, so the only thing I did was ask God with all my strength to help me take care of her so that she could be born healthy. I immediately called my husband to tell him what the doctor had told me. He was very concerned, and could not believe the terrible news since the pregnancy until then had gone normally. He thought that we would lose our daughter.

Arriving at the hospital specializing in preterm births, I was injected with corticosteroids that help accelerate the development of the lungs in premature babies which increases the chance of survival in these types of births; the lungs are vital organs that end up developing toward the end of pregnancy. These steroids have a big advantage for babies born between 25 and 33 weeks of pregnancy. Two injections are applied, with a space of 24 hours between each one. These substances travel through the mother until they reach the baby.

I was put in a room equipped to follow the pregnancy for women who must remain in absolute rest and with medical monitoring at all times until the moment of birth.

Several days passed, in which I could not get out of bed at all, literally at all, much less make any significant effort--nothing that could cause contractions. They were very difficult and stressful days, and it was emotionally and physically exhausting to be lying down all the time with the fear that any movement I made could affect my baby. In addition, there was significant suffering from severe pain in the back from remaining in the same position in bed.

My husband stayed with me some nights after work. It was difficult for him to cross the border, since the lines are normally too long to cross to the United States, and the doctors did not really know how much longer my pregnancy would last. For this reason, he tried to cross the border and stay as long as possible at the hospital to be at the birth of our daughter that could happen any day, while he still attempted going to work.

As the days passed, I listened to doctors and nurses' comment that there were women who managed to successfully extend their pregnancies by maintaining full rest--some even went to full term. There were cases that even with ruptured membranes, and without amniotic fluid in the womb, they managed to extend their pregnancies full term. They also explained to me that every day and week that the baby stayed inside the mother made a huge difference in the child's chances of survival, that is, being born with a better chance of living without chronic problems.

Approximately the third day of being hospitalized in bed, and despite taking all the necessary care I should have, I began to lose amniotic fluid. By this time, I was already quite anguished. It seemed that there had been a small hole in the amniotic sac through which it began to empty little by little, and the slightest movement I made, the more liquid escaped. The amniotic sac is the membrane bag that contains the fluid in which the embryos are found, developing and growing until their birth, and if it breaks prematurely and empties completely, the fetus runs the risk of not developing correctly or reaching the point of losing life inside the womb.

Even when this precious liquid was leaking, the doctors remained optimistic, telling me that we were fine, and that as long as it remained within me, the baby would continue to develop, so the goal would be to lengthen the time of the pregnancy as much as possible. If the baby managed to reach 27 weeks, the probability of being born and having a life without problems was greatly increased. Doctors and nurses also told us that girls statistically have a better chance of survival than boys. They never explained the scientific reason to me; the truth is that simply knowing it gave me more hope.

Babies born between weeks 26 to 28 are considered extremely preterm. Most babies (80 percent) who reach 26 weeks gestation do survive, while those born at 28 weeks have a 94 percent survival rate. And most babies born after 27 weeks survive with no neurological problems[1].

About seven days after being admitted and at full rest, I began to feel strong contractions, the doctors did a checkup, finding some degree of dilation and there was no longer a way to prevent the baby from being born.

I had a whole mix of feelings: Concern for my little girl's life, at the same time some relief at no longer living under the continuous pressure of being careful not to make any movement or effort to prevent the amniotic fluid from continuing to get lost. I felt safe and somewhat calm with myself because I had done everything possible so my baby could be born, and if I still couldn't lengthen the pregnancy any longer, it was because that was the way it had to be and I had to face it with the best attitude of strength and faith.

The nurses prepared me to go to the delivery room where within a few hours, at about 11:00 p.m.

---

[1] https://www.babycenter.com/baby/premature-babies/whats-the-outlook-for-a-premature-baby-born-at-28-31-33-or-3_10300031

my baby was born by natural birth without any complications, besides the fact of being born almost four months early. Remember I actually had strong contractions, but by having epidural anesthesia it was almost painless. When my daughter was born there was not even a chance to see her, she was immediately taken to the intensive care baby unit, my husband and my family told me that they saw how the medical staff wrapped her in an apparent plastic bag, speeding out to save her life.

Caroline was born at 26 weeks and weighing 820 grams on March 7, 2009.

You have to keep pushing towards those dreams, no matter what setbacks happen.

I was exhausted. I had spent the seven most long and difficult days of my life, unable to move or get up from a bed, with the anguish and worry for my daughter's life, plus physical weariness and severe pains especially in the back. I just needed to rest; they even had to give me very strong medicine to relieve the pain during the following days. I just had a huge need to sleep without constant worrying.

CHAPTER III

When reality exceeds the unimaginable.

The next morning, I was finally able to get up and meet my daughter. I had no idea what that meeting would be like, so I went to the floor where the neonatal intensive unit was, got to her crib and saw her for the first time. It was a very strong impression! So tiny and helpless, connected to so many tubes and devices to keep her alive, with breathing assistance sensors connected all over her little body. It was tremendously shocking and painful to see her so small and so fragile, I had never seen any image of a premature baby. It was almost like seeing an image of a fetus inside the mother's uterus. It was evident to the naked eye that she still lacked development time in order to grow and take on the shape and size of a normal born baby.

As soon as I saw her, I started crying. I remember perfectly that moment. I couldn't carry her; I could only touch her a little, while the nurse tried to comfort me, saying that I had no reason to cry since the baby was fine. I imagine that for the doctors and nurses who work in an intensive care unit, it is perhaps very normal to see these cases, but it was my baby who I had been awaiting with so much love, she was part of my being, I couldn't say anything, I couldn't believe what I was living and I just kept crying without stopping.

I constantly had a feeling of great sadness, even when my husband and I went out to eat near the hospital, only tears came out of me without any consolation. I was in a great deal of pain from having my newborn baby in those conditions.

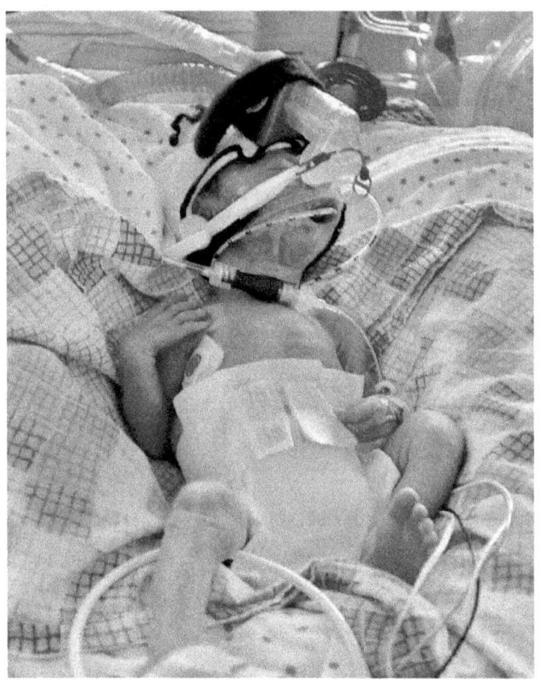

From that first day that Caroline arrived, the doctors informed me that the best thing I could do for her was to breastfeed her, since it was very important to start storing the milk from the first drops that began to come out at the beginning of lactation (called colostrum), and which are attributed wonderful properties for the immune system of all babies, but more importantly for premature babies.

The first food your breasts make is **colostrum** – a sticky, yellow fluid that contains everything your baby needs to transition to life outside your body. Though all infants benefit from colostrum, preterm infants who intake colostrum from the mother's breast have "significantly better health outcomes" than those who do not[2].

With this in mind, I could only think of offering the best that I could to my daughter, and at the time we were talking about her food. So, immediately I started to extract my milk mechanically through a breast pump, which simulates the baby's sucking on the maternal nipple. I followed exactly what they told me: drink plenty of water, extract the milk every three hours, and store it in jars in the refrigerator.

To keep track, on each bottle I wrote the date and time of extraction. At the beginning my production was higher than my daughter's consumption, so it gave me the opportunity to accumulate it in the freezer with its respective labels. Breast milk can last up to three days in the refrigerator, but it can last up to three

[2]https://americanpregnancy.org/breastfeeding/colostrum-the-superfood-for-your-newborn-15379

months in the freezer. This was a great advantage for me in the first months, in order to efficiently and safely store a large supply of food for my daughter. To defrost it, I simply put it in a jar of warm water and in a few minutes it was almost ready, having reached room temperature.

From the first days and throughout the time that my daughter was in the hospital, I took the precaution of taking care of myself so I wouldn't get sick, since I was very concerned that my baby might get the flu or any other illness that could be contagious, because, in that particular year there was a very strong influenza pandemic.

My mental strength made me focus on the fact that I would be healthy for my daughter, since the risk for premature babies of contracting any virus, even a common flu, can be fatal. In addition, if I had gotten sick, I would not have the opportunity to visit her at the hospital. The rules for visitors are very strict for obvious reasons, especially in the neonatal unit, to protect the health and life of these tiny patients. The rest I just put completely in doctors' and God's hands.

But there was one more challenge. The way to feed my little daughter was not easy. In order to give her the breast milk that I extracted from myself with so much effort and care daily, my little one had to ingest it through a nasogastric tube (NG-tube), this is a soft, flexible and extremely thin plastic tube that is inserted through the baby's nose, it goes through the back of the throat, through the esophagus to the stomach. This form of feeding is common in sick or premature babies who are obviously not able to suck or swallow well enough from a bottle or even breastfeed. It is the most efficient and safest way to provide good nutrition to babies in the condition that my daughter was in.

The first days I just wanted to carry her, to have her in my arms, it was my consolation. I was afraid to move her because I felt that I could hurt her, but my biggest fear was the moment of changing her diaper.

As the days went by, I became familiar with the condition of my baby, the medical and nursing staff indicated to me what progress we could expect each week, as well as the time that needed to pass before she could breathe on her own, since due to the immaturity of her brain and spinal cord, which among other functions controls breathing, she suffered episodes of **apnea**.

Apnea is a common abnormality in the breathing of premature babies, pausing it for 15 to 20 seconds while sleeping, decreasing their level of oxygenation and their heart rate. As soon as this happened to my daughter, one of the monitors to which she was connected sounded an alarm and immediately the nurse in turn came to move her little body as a way to make her breathe again. I spent so much time in the neonatal unit that I learned, thanks to the nurses, how to interpret the numbers on the monitors that marked her heart rate, oxygenation level, and other devices that monitored her vital signs.

Several weeks passed before I started to change her tiny diaper. The day also came when they told me that I should help bathe her, and although I was terrified to be moving her, little by little I was gaining confidence. Something that worried me a lot during her bath routine was the fact that all the sensors to which she was connected had to be removed, and I doubted, among other things, if she would continue breathing well, if her heart would continue to beat normally, etc. It was very difficult for me to endure.

There were days when guilt thoughts suddenly came to me, questioning why she was there on that little bed struggling to recover enough to be able to live, while I was in perfect physical condition. I wondered why was this happening? Why was she getting the worst part, being just a life form in the beginning stage. Now I realize that I was strong and healthy because I was going to need all that strength and determination to help my daughter get ahead in life. But at that time I did not see it this way, I had no idea what we would have to go through in the coming years.

CHAPTER IV

Love overcomes pain

Caroline was admitted to the Hospital of San Diego, California while we, my husband and I, continued living on the other side of the border, in Tijuana. So every day, I crossed from Tijuana to San Diego, and back, driving about an hour and a half, to be able to see her and spend the day with her.

Beside my enormous desire to be with her, I knew how important it was to carry her and put her on my chest. Skin-to-skin contact was essential to her evolution. This practice has existed in traditional cultures, interchangeably, and is now understood scientifically as an incredibly beneficial way to welcome a baby, both for the mother and the baby itself. Some scientific studies have shown that skin-to-skin contact causes a release of oxytocin, also known as "the love hormone" in the mother, which among other things, helps the uterus to contract, which reduces the bleeding, and also warms the mother's body, which gives comfort to the baby.

For premature babies that require medical attention right after birth, immediate skin-to-skin contact may not be possible. “But as soon as they are stabilized, we strongly encourage parents to do it,” says Dr. Philip Sunshine, emeritus professor of pediatrics at Stanford Children's Health. Sunshine conducted the benchmark studies on the benefits of skin-to-skin contact for preemies way back in the late 1960s. Now, skin-to-skin contact is part of daily protocol in the NICU. "We think it's so important for healthy development," says Sunshine[3].

This is how I spent my days with my daughter in the hospital, and came home almost at dusk. This was my daily routine, in addition to continuing to extract my milk, simulating the times when a newborn baby would eat.

Sometimes my mom would help me during the week, going to the hospital in the mornings, to carry Caroline, so that I could get some rest and come later. I felt very tired, especially emotionally, since it was extremely painful for me to keep going without being able to take my baby home.

---

[3] https://www.stanfordchildrens.org/en/health-topics/magazine/give-em-some-skin

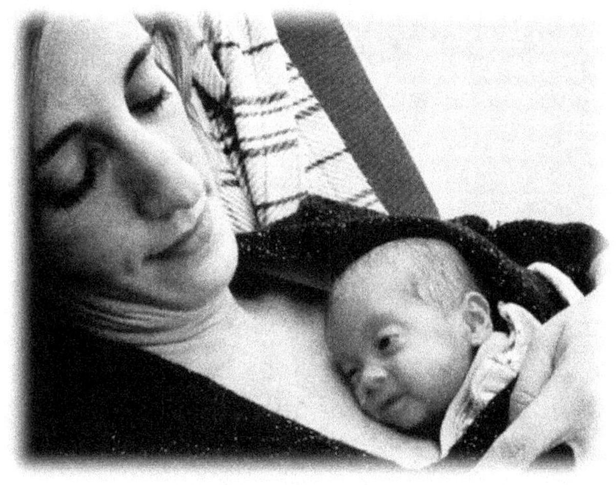

My whole life began to revolve around my daughter. Nothing was more important to me, and the only thing that motivated me was to go see her, be with her and do whatever I had to do, to have her home with me and my husband as soon as possible. Everything else didn't matter, I felt incomplete, broken inside. Even though I had my baby alive, thank God, I think I was in a constant depression; I felt that a part of me was missing. It was inconceivable to be able to lead a normal life, since I didn't feel like doing anything, even eating. What encouraged me to do so was knowing that I had to nourish myself well to produce quality breast milk for her; otherwise, I probably wouldn't have been interested in feeding myself either. Every day I ate with no appetite, the same dish: chicken, rice and vegetables. Nothing made me happy. I thought that any activity other than being with my baby would be betraying her. How could I "enjoy" while she was there in that bed alone with doctors and nurses and away from her parents?

There were people who told me that I had to distract myself too, not just be at home and go to the hospital. Surely, each person reacts differently to these types of situations, but mine was concentrated totally on her. However, now that I look back objectively, I feel those feelings of betraying my daughter were wrong. I wish I could have seen it like that at the time. I think it would have been healthier, both for her and for me, to have found at least some way to make me feel better. Maybe read a book, practice meditation, exercise, seek psychological therapy, or just go out for coffee with friends. Anything that would have helped me deal with the circumstances from another perspective.

So listen to my advice, and if you are going through something similar, something that is not in your hands to change, seek help, seek alternatives, do not let depression dominate you.

This was my personal life routine; but for my husband everything was different. I don't know if it is the fact of having a culturally different origin, or perhaps he had a more practical training in the way of seeing things, but he is more controlled when talking about his emotions and his temperament. Or maybe his feelings and his way of reacting differently from me is due to the nature of his gender. I think that as a woman, things feel different, especially when it comes to the maternal instinct. Whatever the reason, the truth is that for him, it was very important to continue with his life as normally as possible, to continue working his full schedule, with the responsibilities of the position he had in the company where he worked, and above all, get on with his usual social life.

I didn't really know how he was feeling inside. Possibly the work was also a refuge, a distraction from the pain he had inside of him. I don't know. It was a very difficult time in our lives as a couple, with many challenges.

Now I also think that perhaps at that time, for Brian my husband, work could have been his priority, because as the sole provider of the home, he surely felt the pressure to maintain a good family income, to be prepared for any emergency; because we didn't know what medical expenses would come later in Caroline's recovery. At that time when I was fully dedicated to home, the possibility of me working outside the home was unthinkable, since there was nothing more important to me than being with my daughter, besides, thank God, the fact that Brian's income was sufficient to cover all expenses.

My husband and I saw and felt our situation from a totally different perspective. There were days when we ignored each other or argued. I think that my intention to always be in the hospital next to the baby seemed exaggerated to him, while to me, it seemed that his posture was too cold and indifferent to what we were experiencing.

Inevitably there was a rift between us. There was little communication—at times only a bare coexistence. But the weekends that we had time to share in the hospital taking care of our daughter, helped us to reconnect and stay together. Those moments when we left the hospital we would go to lunch or dinner together. These were a great opportunity to get closer. The brief moments made me feel that we were together in this as a couple and as parents sharing this difficult stage. In my constant prayers, I asked God to guide me so that this distancing between us would disappear.

After some time I heard that many couples break up because of this kind of emotional shock. For us, thank God, it was an experience that we managed to overcome, and by which in the end, our relationship strengthened and we remain married today.

A few weeks after she was born, I decided to baptize Caroline. It was very important to me that she receive this blessing. I knew and I know that God was with us, but I had the need to bring a priest to baptize her, with all the formality and symbolism of this Sacrament from my religion. My sister, Elizabeth, helped us with the priest, and my other sister, Rosa

Martha, and Marco, her husband, were the godparents.

In the Neonatal Intensive Unit, not many people can enter, because the area is open and shared with all babies in fragile health conditions; however, the hospital did allow us to celebrate the baptism. For obvious reasons, it was a very brief, but a very special ceremony in which the priest was allowed to approach our daughter's crib to quickly officiate the baptism ritual. Despite the fact that I clung to my faith at all times, when we baptized her I felt an immense peace, as if God were there next to her crib. Possibly for some this does not make any sense, or you don't understand it, but for me, it was something spiritually gratifying.

We never know the path we will have to travel

After spending weeks in the intensive unit, my daughter Caroline was progressing satisfactorily in all the aspects that a premature baby has to go through and overcome--like being able to breathe on her own and have an optimal oxygen level. Thank goodness she had also overcome and eliminated the apnea periods.

Then came the right stage in her maturation in which she could start eating through her mouth, and stop feeding through the nasogastric tube that had been inserted through her nose.

She would now have to learn to eat directly from my breast, so we both began this new adventure of breastfeeding. However, my daughter could not suck out anything.

Trying to make it easier for her to learn to drink her milk directly from my breast, I first tried, with the assistance of the nurses, to use nipple shields, which are adapters or small pieces of silicone that adhere to the mother's nipple, to facilitate suctioning for babies, when they cannot do it on their own. These breastfeeding instruments are very useful in babies with difficulties achieving or maintaining the "latch" of the breast, as in the case of premature babies, who do not have enough force to suck out; because they offer the baby a firm stimulus on the soft palate, which helps to extract breast milk more effectively and for a longer time.

After trying to breastfeed my daughter with the help of nipple shields, we saw, unfortunately, that they did not work for us. So they suggested the use of special bottles for premature babies. These are very small and have a very soft pacifier, so that the baby can use little force, and suction is easier. With them, Caroline managed to take only a few milliliters, and then we supplemented her food through the probe.

I thought optimistically that it would be a matter of a few days for her to learn to sip, and to start taking her food without any major problem. But time passed, and after four weeks during which the nurses and I tried different methods and techniques to get her to drink her milk, we could not enable her to take enough by mouth to be able to nourish her and receive liquids and calories necessary to grow, so it was necessary to go to medical intervention.

The doctors in charge of the Neonatal Intensive Unit ordered X-rays to be taken to detect any possible physical obstruction in the digestive system, which prevented her from eating. She also had esophageal pH monitoring to measure acidity in the esophagus, inserting a fine tube through the mouth to reach it. This probe was connected to a device that monitored the acidity for a period of 24 hours, thus having a long measurement record.

The diagnosis after this study was **infantile reflux**, or gastro **esophageal reflux** (GER). Infant reflux occurs when food backs up (refluxes) from a baby's stomach, causing the baby to spit up. Sometimes called gastroesophageal reflux (GER), the condition is rarely serious and becomes less common as a baby gets older. It's unusual for infant reflux to continue after age 18 months. In infants, the ring of muscle between the esophagus and the stomach — the lower esophageal sphincter (LES) — is not yet fully mature. That allows stomach contents to flow backward. Eventually, the LES will open only when your baby swallows and will remain tightly closed at other times, keeping stomach contents where they belong.[4]

In the hospital, they explained to me that in many cases, as the infant matures, this digestive disorder is completely overcome, and once the patient feels better, the patient gradually accepts more food through the mouth. They never defined an estimated timeframe for this to happen. Despite this, during the months that my newborn daughter was admitted to the hospital, she retained her food very well, even if it was not orally, and she continued to gain weight at an adequate rate. The nurses who assisted her 24 hours a day indicated in their reports that there were very few occasions in which she vomited, and that when it did occur, she did so in small quantities.

Probably for these reasons, the doctors did not consider it important to continue investigating if there was any other problem that caused her aversion to receiving food through her mouth, attributing it only to the diagnosed reflux, according the studies they had done.

Almost three months in the hospital, the only thing that kept her there was the problem of not eating by mouth. Otherwise, her development was going very well. She already had the approximate weight of a

[4] https://www.mayoclinic.org/diseases-conditions/infant-acid-reflux/symptoms-causes/syc-20351408

newborn baby, full term of pregnancy, so they gave me two options to be able to discharge her. One was to leave in her the nasogastric tube that she had from the nostril to the stomach; with which she had been fed since she was a newborn. If we decided on this alternative, I would have to train myself to know how to reinstall it in case my daughter accidentally pulled it out with her little hands, or for any other reason it moved out of place. In case this happened, I would have to be very careful at home, to reinstall it correctly, making sure that the tube was placed, reaching the stomach, and not the lungs. Although they are separate ducts, they are very close to each other and can easily be confused.

The other option they offered us, if we were to take her home, was to do a gastrostomy, which is a surgical procedure in which a feeding tube, or gastrostomy tube, is inserted through the abdomen, to transport the nutrition directly to the stomach, staying there permanently. That way, we wouldn't have to worry about it being moved or disconnected so easily.

When the gastrostomy option was explained to us, I did not want to go too deep to understand it well, nor did I want to visualize what this process of feeding at home with my baby would be like, because it did not give me any peace of mind to put my daughter in surgery, to cut a hole in the stomach and insert a permanent probe.

I was so overwhelmed with the information we received; at the same time we wanted to take Caroline home so strongly that the only thing that was clear to us was that this last alternative was the safest. I was terrified that if there was a need to fit her nasogastric tube, I might do it wrong and put it in her lungs instead of her stomach. I didn't want to take any chances at home, accidentally bothering her or hurting her. My husband and I had a decision to make. If not, our daughter would stay in the hospital for an indefinite period, until she could eat through her mouth.

So, after analyzing the two options in detail, and weighing the pros and cons of each one, we opted for gastrostomy, which, even though we considered it a very drastic measure, was the only way to guarantee that our baby could finally be at home in our care, taking in enough nutrients to continue growing safely.

Although I was happy that I would soon be able to have my daughter at home, I was very afraid and uncertain that I would have to go to an operating room. I didn't know what the process was going to be like or the repercussions for my daughter having that probe in her body.

It was another extremely sad experience for me. Seeing my little girl come out of surgery, with a hole in her belly, and with that plastic tube sticking out of her little body. Once again I felt a great pain, a great sorrow to see her like this. Deep down, I was very concerned, so much so that something inside told me that it was not the right or necessary path for my daughter.

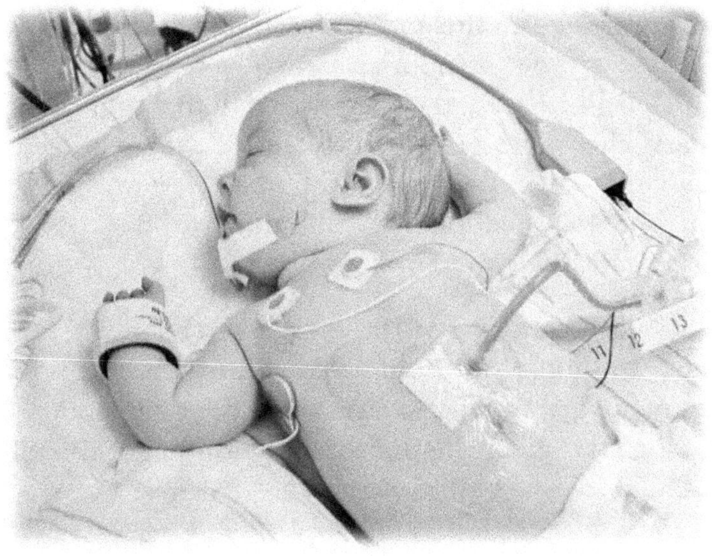

"Every adversity, every failure, every heartache carries with it the seed of an equal or greater benefit." Napoleon Hill

After the doctors made sure that the gastric tube was working correctly, that my daughter was accepting the milk without problems, and that there was no reaction or rejection, two days after the surgery, she was finally discharged from the hospital!

Before leaving the hospital, they taught me how to keep the area around the tube clean, and how to pass the food little by little, manually, using a huge syringe that was connected to the end of the tube, allowing gravity to cause a flow of nourishment down to my baby's stomach. The food passing through the tube lasted almost the same period that it would take to feed a newborn baby through the mouth. They warned me that the inserted tube would have to be changed periodically by a surgeon.

The day came at three months of age when the amount of milk that I extracted with the breast pump was no longer enough to satisfy my baby's appetite, so I had to start giving her more baby formula, so that she could be satisfied after each meal.

Sometimes it is very stressful for some women, especially when we have premature babies, not to produce a large amount of milk in the lactation stage, because doctors insist strongly that the best food for our children is breast milk, and when for some reason we cannot produce enough, we get to feel pressured, or worse, we think we are failing as mothers. But there is no need to feel that way. We must remember that each case is different, and that what may work for some mothers at this stage, may not for others, and that we must also be calm in knowing that, despite the fact that some of us are not able to produce the amount we would like to give our baby, they can continue to benefit from the nutrition of breast milk, even if it must be supplemented with baby formula.

CHAPTER V

A grand change in my life

Finally after three long months we were able to take our daughter home!

So the long awaited day arrived. We left the hospital happy to finally be able to take our beautiful girl with us, but I was feeling a little nervous. Now I was going to be alone, without any doctor or nurse near me to assist me in whatever situation arose; so we opted to stay with my sister Elizabeth, who lived in San Diego. We wanted to be close to the hospital until we felt more comfortable and safe with our daughter.

On the second day of having her with us, when I was feeding her milk, and following all the instructions received at the hospital, suddenly Caroline began to vomit everything. I was very scared; I didn't know what was happening. At that moment I was carrying her with one arm, and with the other, I had the syringe with which I was giving her the milk little by little, just as they had explained to me that I should do. I still remember perfectly that day, I got very nervous. My baby wouldn't stop vomiting, though my sister tried to help me. I just held her and saw an impressive volume of formula coming out of her mouth without stopping. Just as it had entered her stomach, it came out completely. This would be the first of so many episodes that I experienced with Caroline.

I immediately spoke to the clinic to make an appointment and take her to see the gastroenterologist who had treated her from the Neonatal Intensive Unit. Being a patient with problems in the digestive tract, my daughter required a doctor with this medical specialty to monitor her progress, and we had decided to continue with that same doctor, in addition to the family pediatrician. He simply commented that what had caused the vomiting was the same reflux that had already been diagnosed before, so no further clinical studies were conducted to find the explanation for her vomiting.

Simply, I was not satisfied with this diagnosis, or with the explanation about the cause of the vomiting. I was wondering why this was happening precisely after the tube was inserted in her stomach. I saw a lot of coincidence that this was happening right after she had the surgery. During her stay in the hospital, Caroline had vomited, but very rarely. My perception was that the intensity of these events increased after the gastrostomy. I started to do a little research on gastric tubes on the internet, and somewhere I read that these tubes could cause reflux to exacerbate, given that to insert and fix the gastric tube, they stretch a part of the stomach to join it with seams to the skin of the abdomen, causing stiffness, without the possibility of moving naturally to prevent the tube from moving and becoming detached.

Even when I discussed with the doctors what I had read, they never took it as a possible cause of her vomiting. To me on the other hand, it was something very clear that, after the operation to insert the gastrostomy feeding tube, vomiting began to occur constantly and in large quantities.

When challenges shape our character

From that day when she vomited for the first time at home, Caroline began to vomit daily after every meal. Feeding her became a superhuman effort, difficult and stressful, since apart from putting the food from the syringe into the tube, I had to figure out how to keep her almost sitting up, without moving her, to try to keep the food in the stomach, and wait in almost the same vertical position for the digestion to take place.

At first I carried the baby with one arm, and with the opposite hand I was applying the food, but as the weeks passed, it occurred to me to place her in a baby carrier, the kind by which you can adjust the angle of inclination. This was very useful particularly at night, which was when I was more tired, since she had to sit at an inclination to be fed. I arranged several little blankets around her body, to ensure that she was more comfortable, and at the same time they supported her little head when she fell asleep.

My husband and I have always commented that, despite having gone through so much discomfort and constant unrest of indigestion, which I surely know she felt, my daughter remained calm, didn't cry much, and was also very good at sleeping. The nurses at the hospital referred to her as Sleeping Beauty, because she slept a lot, and they told Brian and me that she was a very quiet girl, that it was a characteristic of her personality, and that she would surely be that way when she grew up. She was a baby who rarely threw tantrums or cried, and as she grew older and showed traits of her character, we began to recognize that she was also a very sweet and tender girl.

Each meal was a long ritual. First I had to extract the milk from my breast with the electric breast pump; then I had to feed my daughter very slowly, always tending to keep her seated. But despite all these cares, my daughter continued to vomit daily, and sometimes all the milk she drank; so I had to feed her again, even a little more, calculating what she could have vomited. I think with the experience gained, I could already tell how many milliliters she had vomited. In fact, over the months, it occurred to me to always have a plastic container by my side when I fed her, to immediately bring it closer to her as soon as she started coughing and coughing, because that was a signal that the food was coming. I would put the plastic container out of Caroline's sight to avoid any mental association between the container and the urge to vomit.

My life began to revolve around how and when to feed my baby, to maintain her proper growth and evolution. All the activities of my daughter, as well as mine, of the home or whatever arose, had to be scheduled around the hours of feeding my daughter, always respecting the necessary time of rest, which lasted between half an hour or an hour, to avoid as much as possible the vomiting of the food she had just eaten.

During this stage of my daughter's life, I continued making great effort to maintain lactation for several months, even though I had to extract my milk with a machine. I saw it as a great resource to help her receive the antibodies and nutritive properties that only breast milk has. For me, despite the strong fatigue, it was a blessing to be able to do it; I felt that it was the only good thing I personally could offer her, given her condition. As I mentioned earlier, even in small amounts, my girl continued to receive the benefits of this nutrient.

On one occasion I had the opportunity to see the wonder of the benefits of breast milk, when I got sick with a very bad flu, which caused a sore throat and an unstoppable cough. I was able to continue caring for my daughter, who, thank God (and surely by consuming breast milk), remained immune to my illness.

The doctors advised me to continue trying to feed her by mouth, but every day the number of milliliters that my daughter accepted with a bottle was less, because the vomiting happened daily, even after two hours of having taken her food, and sometimes up to more than three times a day. She vomited all the food that had been given to her through the gastric tube. My mother's intuition made me think that my little girl was not digesting her food normally.

Simultaneously, she continued with periodic visits and medical check-ups, but these were irrelevant, since they were only to monitor her growth and weight, but her problem of dislike to food was not addressed in any way, nor did they provide any solution for the usual vomiting. The gastroenterologist told me the usual; that Caroline continued to vomit due to the reflux, and that as her organs grew and matured, this disorder would diminish.

This was perhaps the most difficult phase, the first six months at home. I really lived exhausted, both emotionally and physically, especially at night, because of everything involved in being able to feed her; in addition to doing it with the same frequency as that of a newborn baby--every three hours. The time to rest between one feeding and another was very short and the nights became longer and tiring, without my being able to sleep. The ritual every night included extracting my milk, feeding it through the tube, and above all, making sure that my baby retained as much food as possible, without vomiting; and if she did, feed her again.

For any mother, the first months are heavy due to the lack of hours of sleep--for me it was even more so. My exhaustion became such a critical situation that my in-laws and some of my husband's aunt and uncle took the initiative to help us financially, to cover the cost of the services of a night nurse, with the intention of alleviating a little of the heavy physical exhaustion. It turned out to be a great relief as it allowed me to recover a bit by enjoying longer periods of sleep.

Having a nurse at night for a month and a half was undoubtedly a great help. However, I was not going to sleep completely calm. I was always on the lookout for my daughter—especially when it was the turn of one of the two nurses who attended during this stage. One of them was excellent; seeing her work gave me enough peace of mind to relax my sleep. But when it was the night for the other nurse, I went to bed very restless. On several occasions I had to get up to hear my daughter cough constantly and then vomit. I think maybe the nurse poured the food very quickly through the gastric tube, because it coincided that just when it was her turn to take care of my daughter, my girl vomited almost everything she had taken, so those nights I rested, but never enough to disconnect myself completely.

Upon the arrival home, I slept at night on the couch in the living room next to the baby carrier where I put her, but as the months went by, and seeing that there was no improvement, I realized unfortunately that it would take more time to have a stable or normal healthy situation. For this reason I had to add a bed in her room, to sleep next to her, and thus be able to take care of her that she didn't vomit; and if she did, supervise that it wouldn't drown her, by carrying her in an upright position. Then I had to change her into clean clothes and give her a little more food again; practically, in addition to being her mother, I became my daughter's nurse 24 hours a day.

So this is how the first months passed, extracting my milk with the special machine, feeding it through the tube every three hours, sleepless nights, visits to the doctors and occupational therapies assigned to her as part of her treatment, in order for her to learn to accept food orally.

These types of therapies exist to help patients to carry out any activity by themselves, be it personal care, work or even a fun activity, in order to increase functional independence, increase development and prevent disability which, in the case of my daughter, was eating through the mouth.

One morning I was shocked to death. As I was changing Caroline, I noticed that the tube had come loose from her stomach, exposing the hole in the abdomen where it was inserted; the milk that was still in her stomach began to spill. I was really shocked at what I saw. I didn't know what to do, as I had not been warned that this could happen. The only thing that occurred to me at that moment, without having given it much thought, was to cover the hole with gauze and run immediately to the hospital. Upon arriving at the emergency room, the medical staff, who treated me very calmly, questioned whether I didn't know how to reinsert it, and told me that I should learn to do it at home, or else I would be running to the hospital every time this happened, because either way, the tube would have to be exchanged for a new one approximately every three months.

So when it came to the next gastric tube change, I went to the surgeon's office and asked the doctor and nurse who was assisting him, to show me step by step how to change and insert the tube myself at home correctly and safely to my baby, Caroline. At the same time, I had to learn to overcome the fear I felt of seeing her exposed belly, when I removed the tube to place the new one.

It might sound like a relatively easy thing to do, but to me it wasn't. I had never experienced a similar situation in my life, and I never imagined being able to do something like that. Despite this, I had no other option but to arm myself with courage and learn how to do it.

As time went by and with practice, I already had my own technique to change the tube, although I have to admit that I never stopped feeling a very strange sensation every time I did it. It gave me a chill through my body when I inserted the new tube, as if I was cutting off her belly. I don't think I have the stomach for that kind of medical work, which for doctors and nurses is an everyday task.

Nothing prepares us to live the trials of life, but if they are there, it is because we can overcome them

After having managed to give my daughter nine months of breast milk in some quantity, I decided to stop extracting it, and as soon as she stopped consuming it, I noticed that she started to get sick, increasing the frequency of vomiting, because when she got a cold or cough, she vomited her food much more easily. The accumulation of mucus made her problem more acute. This is why I avoided taking her out of the house. We hardly ever visited public places, as any mom would normally do. My friends and family believed that I was overprotective of my daughter, but no one really knew the stress and fatigue that I experienced from day to day, at home. If for some reason my husband and I decided to go out as a family, it was a very stressful logistics protocol, because we had to be aware of several factors, such as scheduling the times to feed her, waiting for a sufficient time of rest so that she wouldn't vomit, and then be able to transfer her by car, wherever we went, so that the movements of the road wouldn't make her vomit, or continue vomiting, if it had been one of those days.

The gastroenterologist who treated Caroline, seeing that she was already just over nine months old without having yet been able to accept the food orally and that the vomiting also increased in frequency, proposed to us as a solution performing a **Nissen Fundoplication**, and avoid her digestive system's greater loathing to food.

Fundoplication is a common surgical technique for the treatment of gastro esophageal reflux, which until then was the diagnosis that had been given to my daughter. Laparoscopic anti-reflux surgery for GERD may involve a procedure to reinforce the lower esophageal sphincter, called **Nissen fundoplication**. In this procedure, the surgeon wraps the top of the stomach around the lower esophagus after reducing the hiatal hernia, if present. This reinforces the lower esophageal sphincter, making it less likely that acid will back up in the esophagus[5]. By strengthening the sphincter, it would make it impossible for my baby to vomit food.

I was totally opposed to this surgery, be it maternal instinct, intuition, or simply God's guidance, but I knew that this was not the solution for my daughter. Something inside me told me that I had to keep looking for the right solution to help her, and I felt a great sense of helplessness to perceive that a specialist doctor like the one who treated us, was not trying hard enough to find a way to help the patient. He only limited himself to the diagnosis obtained from clinical studies carried out when my daughter was born, and nothing more.

I felt very frustrated as if my arms were tied, but I was determined to help my daughter, so I decided to get a second opinion from another gastroenterologist, because I assumed that another point of view could contribute to finding the true reason for which my daughter refused food. Her pediatrician suggested another specialist she knew, and I followed her recommendation.

We all possess the faculty of intuition, but I think that when it comes to what we want the most it is even stronger

---

[5] https://www.mayoclinic.org/diseases-conditions/gerd/multimedia/gerd-surgery/img-20006950

The new doctor was within the same gastroenterology clinic at the Children's Hospital. The truth is that we didn't find much difference from the previous specialist, except that he was less drastic in his solution proposals. He suggested that we not operate on my daughter, and that we wait longer, since many patients from the age of three begin to show improvement due to the maturation of their organs, and that in many cases it is observed that the reflux diminishes, so we chose to follow this advice and be patient, waiting even longer for the reflux to resolve naturally.

We let the months go by, and in the process we continued to take Caroline to her occupational feeding therapies.

Every week we attended the Children's Therapy Clinic in San Diego, with a therapist who introduced Caroline to different types of food, also exposing her to different cutlery of different textures and materials, to see if some of them might be accepted into her mouth. Her aversion to food was so strong that we celebrated it as a great achievement to see her put any of these spoons into her mouth by herself, even when she had no food in it.

Food with varied textures and colors was also used, so that she would get used to touching and feeling them; the therapy also included the use of instruments that vibrated, and that in turn had some attractive figure for young children. The medical personnel passed them around their mouths, to stimulate their lower jaw muscles, ensuring that my daughter created a positive association of food, with a fun and pleasant feeling. They imagined this might cure her aversion to the food. It was extremely important that her mind didn't associate the food with something unpleasant, such as nausea and vomiting.

Sometimes my daughter did begin try something, but then she wouldn't try it anymore, there was no progress. On the contrary, it seemed that the rejection of food was increasing. The more that time passed, the more difficult it became for her to agree to eat something. I was very concerned to know that there are extreme cases, where children with this problem can reach youth without having accepted food orally, and that they continue to eat 100% through the gastric tube.

CHAPTER VI

The frantic search for solutions

In our despair during the first year of Caroline's life, my husband and I looked for different alternatives such as homeopathic medicine. I knew that in this type of medicine the treatment was with natural substances, and I thought that, although it would not help her much, it could not harm her either. We sought the advice of a doctor who prescribed a treatment with drops, which had to be taken naturally by the mouth, which were to help her stomach function properly, improving her digestion and supposedly also help control reflux. This medicine had to be taken before every meal; her stomach had to be totally empty, that was the only way my daughter could take the drops without vomiting. We gave her this medicine for a couple of months, but we didn't have great results.

Another option that we tried was suggested by my husband's aunt and uncle, who recommended us to some alternative medicine specialists who had treated their grandchildren, through a method known as **NAET**, (Nambudripad Allergy Elimination Technique). This technique is a non-invasive, drug free, natural solution to alleviate allergies of all types and intensities using a blend of selective energy balancing, testing and treatment procedures from acupuncture/acupressure, allopathy, chiropractic, nutritional, and kinesiological disciplines of medicine[6].

Surprisingly, with this treatment, excellent results were achieved in the cure of severe allergies that were found in my husband's nephews, such as allergies from eating peanuts and strawberries, which made me suspect that it would probably work for Caroline, under the belief that the cause of what was happening to her was related to some type of allergy, so we decided to perform this procedure. I traveled with her to Salt Lake City, Utah, where my husband's relatives lived, to treat her in the same clinic specializing in this method, where they had treated their grandchildren with great success. (Later I will explain how this technique was applied). Brian stayed in Tijuana because of his job.

The treatment process was long, requiring an estimated two months to be completed properly. But it was not possible to finish it, because it would have been very difficult for me to spend those months alone, my daughter and I, in a city I did not know, living in the house of my husband's relatives. Even though they treated us wonderfully, it was not the same as being in my own home. So we were only there for a week, in which we could hardly note any improvement, and I decided to go home.

---

[6] https://www.naet.com/about/what-is-naet/

Flying back to San Diego, we made a stopover in Phoenix, Arizona. While we waited inside the plane, I sat my daughter in the seat to rearrange the diaper bag and the things we needed to continue our trip, and in an instant that I turned to move things, Caroline fell to the ground. Despite the very short distance between the seat and the floor of the plane, Caroline appeared to have injured herself. As soon as I picked her up from the floor and laid her on the seat to check her, I noticed that she was not moving her arms and that she was very still, and I could tell that something was not right. I was very scared and thought that something serious might have happened to her internally. Then in a matter of seconds I had to ask myself, was I continuing my flight to San Diego without saying anything? Or should I tell the flight attendant? The only thing that made me consider continuing the flight is that she was not crying.

I decided to ask for help right there, and even if I wanted to stay in the plane, they no longer allowed me to continue the flight, so we had to get off the plane. They sent an ambulance to transport Caroline from the airport to the hospital and after being looked at by the doctor and taking X-rays of her, they found a fracture in her forearm. They did not cast her on that occasion, but they did immobilize her arm with a splint. After several hours of waiting in the hospital, and feeling completely exhausted, I found a hotel near the airport for the night. This last event was one of the many adventures we went through in search of a cure for my daughter.

Upon arriving in San Diego, my daughter was again checked out by the doctors for her injury at Children's Hospital, where she had always been treated. They put a cast on her and told us that she should have it on for six weeks.

After Caroline recovered from this fracture, my husband and I decided NAET was worth a try, so we looked at where my daughter could continue the treatment she had started in Utah. I was sure that I would find one close to home, someone who knew this practice. Then I remembered that when we were in Utah, the doctor we visited told us that Devi Nambudripad, the doctor who created this treatment, was in the city of Los Angeles, California, so I looked for her information on the internet and found her clinic. Even though we hadn't seen much improvement this week in Utah, I was hopeful that it might work once treatment was completed. If she had already helped other patients, why not Caroline? I felt like it was the only option I had at the time.

Despite living in frustration, despair and exhaustion, both emotionally and physically looking for a cure for my daughter's health; it was never an alternative for me to sit idly by, waiting lightheartedly to see if doctors could figure things out. I was not satisfied with letting more time pass and waiting passively, without seeing any progress in my daughter's health.

I believed that the way to find the solution to my daughter's problem was to keep moving, take action, trying, looking for alternatives in one way or another. I always kept the faith that there must be a solution, for my Caroline's condition.

"Perseverance is the basis of all actions." -Lao Tzu

So for the next two months, we were going back and forth to Los Angeles twice a week to treat her. Despite taking me almost four hours of driving a day, this time Caroline did finish the entire NAET treatment, as directed by its creator. But sadly, my daughter didn't indicate any improvement in her health either. On these trips there were times when I had to stop in the middle of the road, because my little girl would vomit on the way, and I had to clean both her and the seat she was sitting on.

This method was, as I already mentioned, completely alternative, different and perhaps outside of any common procedure in traditional medicine. It consisted of trying one by one the foods or substances that could cause allergies in patients. These substances were kept in small containers, and the patient was holding them in a hand with the arm up and pointing forward, while the doctor tried to lower the arm by pushing it down. If she managed to lower her arm, this indicated that the substance was an allergen for the patient, which meant that the patient had to avoid eating this substance for a few days after the day of treatment. The next healing step in the session was massages that were given along the patient's back, touching all the vertebrae of the spine.

As my daughter was very young, the test of the containers and possible allergens was done through me. With one hand I held the containers raising my arm so that the doctor tried to lower it, while with my other hand I touched my girl's abdomen. I understand that it may sound very unscientific, and even incredible to some people, but we had the testimony of our relatives, who assured us that this allergy treatment had worked with great success. The difference with them was that my husband's nephews who had been treated were older than Caroline and the tests had been done directly on them.

Our purpose was to rule out the possibility that an allergy could be causing Caroline's nausea and vomiting. However, from the beginning the doctors had never mentioned any allergies--they merely repeated and insisted on the same diagnosis of reflux.

I deduced that the problem could be related to an allergic reaction, because I noticed that my daughter was not digesting food at all. Her face reflected the nausea caused by the food, and it seemed even instinctive for her to cough until she managed to vomit and expel all that food that caused her so much discomfort.

My family tried to help in some way to find solutions. Therefore, another of the medical opinions that we discovered was that of a doctor specializing in pediatric gastroenterology. It was recommended to me by my older sister, Rosa Martha. He was the doctor of my sister's child and periodically attended to her children in Tijuana. We visited him, but again, we left the consultation with very few new possibilities that could help my daughter.

All these attempts, treatments and consultations that I made to find something that would help her to be fed by mouth, were always at par with the therapies recommended by the Children's Hospital for cases of premature patients and with gastric tubes, such as in physical therapy, very important for the evolution of your motor skills, because being a premature baby, she could present some delay in the progress of her psychomotor system, and of course, the occupational therapy that we always had for feeding.

On her first year, we performed a symbolic Baptism ceremony, but now it was in the Church, since the sacrament itself had been received in the hospital. I wanted to have a ceremony like this in the traditional way in our religion, perhaps more for me than for my daughter, because I longed to live a joyful and stress-free celebration, and I saw it as a good opportunity to celebrate her first birthday.

We had a very nice party at my parents' house, with the visit of my in-laws who traveled from Alabama to celebrate with their granddaughter, as well as the company of family and close friends. These types of experiences were like a pause from what we were living day to day. They were opportunities to enjoy Caroline's life, which, although under difficult circumstances, we still had her with us, thank God.

Perhaps you may wonder why I did not consult other specialists in traditional medicine. Even today, writing this book, I ask myself the same question. How is it that I did not demand more in-depth studies that would lead us to correctly diagnose her? The only answer I can give myself is that she was being treated by specialists in pediatric gastroenterology, who belonged to one of the best children's hospitals in the United States, and at that time I couldn't think of where else she could have gone, outside of this group of specialized doctors dedicated to everything related to the digestive system.

We cannot and should not live thinking about the "would haves" so I can only accept that the decisions we made regarding my daughter's treatment were the best options that were presented to us at that time, and that, if things happened positively, it is because that is how they should have happened.

"Accepting is not resignation, but nothing makes you lose more energy than resisting and fighting against a situation that you cannot change." -Dalai Lama

There is an aspect in this whole experience, which perhaps I have not clearly mentioned, and which was also a great challenge that I always had to face: the English language. Although my husband is American, and I speak and understand English, it was very difficult for me to fully understand all the explanations and indications that doctors in the United States have told me, and it was much more complicated to make me understand, because being realistic, I am not fluent in the language 100%, and even less in the context of medical terms. In some clinics and hospitals there are bilingual personnel to assist in cases like this, but when I came to rely on them, I realized that their translations were not entirely clear and precise. Sometimes I believed that I could explain my ideas in a better way, so I preferred to make the effort to communicate without a simultaneous translator, thinking that this way I would have a better opportunity to convey my exact concerns, and patiently seek to understand what the doctors and therapists explained to me.

Throughout her first years, Caroline underwent various tests and reviews, which are done on premature babies to follow up and monitor their development. Thank God, she was showing satisfactory progress in each one of them. Some were for the heart, others for tracking the weight and height; always measuring according to the adjusted age, which is, subtracting the months of gestation that should have been spent in the mother's womb, to more objectively compare their development with that of a child born at term.

Other tests that were done were to monitor her neurological development, allowing her to do different activities to measure the degree of evolution she was taking.

After a period of having completed the recommended physical therapy sessions at the specialized Children's Clinic, I realized that Caroline was not showing any progress, so I decided to stop taking her. I looked for other options within my city (Tijuana), and I found a local EARLY STIMULATION program, which helped her a lot. The creator is a highly accredited person in the field. She had a local television program, and she gave training courses in her own technique to some people to broadcast it in different places within the city.

With the help of this program Caroline finally managed to crawl, and shortly after she learned how to do it, at the age of one and a half years, she surprisingly began to walk. With these classes she was able to advance a lot in her gross motor coordination, and to catch up with some movements that due to her age she should already perform. Along with Caroline's progress, these sessions were very beneficial for me, because we joined many mothers with babies, which allowed me to share experiences, socialize, talk with them and above all, distract my mind, getting out of the routine of stressful occasions at home.

CHAPTER VII

The right path

"Ask and it will be given to you; seek and you will find; knock and the door will be opened to you."

I was still desperate to get my daughter to accept food through the mouth, since she had not been able to eliminate the daily vomiting; however, as is often the case, when someone 'searches' and asks with great faith, sooner or later, she 'finds.'

I continued taking Caroline to occupational therapy, until one fine day, talking with the therapist who was helping her to learn to eat; she told me that in her opinion, it would be good to reconsider as a solution the fundoplication, which was the surgical intervention that the gastroenterologist had previously proposed. I think that even she could see that those almost two years of sessions with her did not imply any progress. Despite not understanding 100% of what she was saying due to the language, I managed to understand this much: She was recommending that I consult the case with a surgeon she knew. She said she knew that the doctor was performing this operation with very good results. The therapist assured me that she had witnessed considerable progress during her therapies in the patients who had had this intervention with him.

According to her experience, the therapist had observed that the children who had had reflux problems and vomiting, not only showed great improvement, but also did not present the side effect of the gag reflex, which appeared very commonly after this operation, so the patients gradually accepted eating orally with success.

Even though I was still reluctant to do this procedure on Caroline, I contacted the surgeon the therapist told me about, and we made the appointment. I thought there would be nothing to lose by going to see him. When visiting him in his office, he explained to me in detail what this surgical intervention would be like and how it would help my daughter to stop vomiting; He made a very good impression on me as a doctor.

Caroline was almost two years old, during which life had been a constant struggle to keep food in her stomach, in addition to the fact that I always had to be on the lookout when feeding her again every time she vomited. Added to this was the constant anguish and concern that she would obtain sufficient nutrition for her physical development, which, as I had already mentioned, somehow was proceeding correctly, thank God -at the cost of boatloads of stress and discipline to feed her at any cost. My focus was always to ensure that my daughter had optimal growth and development.

Despite this entire difficult situation that we lived with Caroline every day, I left the consultation not completely convinced that fundoplication was the option to solve my daughter's health problem.

My husband and I reached the point of having lost all hope, so desperate and frustrated that we could not do anything to change the situation. It was already two years, and our daughter could not eat normally!

Insist, persist, resist, and never give up

I don't remember the exact day, but after my husband and I discussed it, and having exhausted all the alternatives, we decided to go back to the surgeon to schedule the surgery. This time we both attended the consult. I wanted to be completely sure that there was a perfectly clear communication using the English language, by the presence of my husband. It was a critical situation to be there with my daughter in my arms, and to listen to the doctor talk about all the details of the procedure, and while he was doing it, something inside of me was screaming that this was not the way. I couldn't hold back anymore and started crying. Seeing me like this the surgeon told me that if I was not sure about permitting the surgery, I should not do it. He was a cold doctor, not very gentle, but I think he was sensible. After he told me, I couldn't take it anymore, and I began to vent with tears in my eyes, telling him about everything we had experienced in these two years of Caroline's life; that they had not carried out any type of more detailed study to check inside her organs; that doctors had never done an endoscopy, and that the only studies that had been done for the diagnosis had been when she was born in the hospital; just to measure acidity, and some x-rays, but nothing else. I told him how throughout all the consultations and treatments, the diagnosis was always been confined to reflux, but precisely because nobody inquired further into the reason for her condition, I was not convinced that it was only reflux.

I considered that there were not enough clinical reasons for her to undergo fundoplication. After listening to me, the surgeon recommended that we consult a colleague of his, a specialist in gastroenterology; he gave me his details and we left with new hope. I called as soon as possible to make an appointment. This would be the third gastroenterologist that we would consult at that same clinic.

On the day of the appointment with the recommended gastroenterologist, I saw a doctor who I felt was more human and kind than the previous ones. I briefly explained my daughter's history, and her first comment was: "We are going to do an endoscopy." Hearing that someone would finally do this study for my daughter, it was like hearing the voice of God telling me “now we are on the right path.” I felt great happiness inside me knowing that there would finally be a medical examination from within, and then we could see what was really going on in her digestive system. I am not a doctor or anything related to that profession, but I am a mother. My instincts and common sense told me that this was the way to find out what was really going on in my Caroline's body.

Caroline was already two years old when they performed the endoscopy study, with which they did find signs of reflux, but there was something more relevant. The biggest discovery was a narrowing in the duodenum, which is the first part of the small intestine, where it joins the stomach. This meant that there was an obstruction that prevented food from the stomach to empty properly into the intestine. This condition is known as **duodenal stenosis**, and it is a rare congenital malformation, in which the duodenum has not developed properly. It’s not completely open, and cannot allow the contents of the stomach to pass through. Also during the same study she was subjected to, biopsies were taken throughout her entire digestive tract to analyze the internal tissue.

We finally had the full diagnosis. It was the answer to why so much vomiting after feeding my baby. Now I understood how difficult it was for her stomach to empty itself normally during the digestion process, and then everything made sense to me. The food would go in, reach her stomach and get trapped there, draining very slowly.

I don't even want to imagine what my daughter would have suffered if I had accepted that surgery to close the passage back from her stomach to her esophagus. I thanked God for having enlightened me to deny prior suggestions. It is unimaginable the pain and the horrible sensation that my daughter would have gone through receiving the food, without being able to expel it through her mouth.

Always listen to your inner voice

Once we had this diagnosis that seemed well-determined, we went back to the surgeon, but this time to talk about the corrective surgery for this problem. Unlike the previous consultation, I was feeling very optimistic, and I wanted the duodenal surgery to be as soon as possible to continue my daughter's healing. A few weeks later, the intervention was carried out. I was happy and calm, I had the certainty and faith that from this day on everything would begin to improve; I didn't stop to think about obstacles, nor about the post-operative recovery process.

The operation lasted a couple of hours, in which my husband, my mother and I were in the waiting room, asking God to enlighten the doctor so that everything would go well.

The incision was horizontal, more or less 6 cm, in her abdominal area; the surgeon explained the finding to us: there was tissue obstructing the passage that normally exists between the stomach and the duodenum, confirming what had already been seen in the endoscopy. Despite the fact that this space was not completely closed, as in some cases, Caroline had only a 2mm opening of the duodenum, and obviously, this was the reason why she was vomiting. Her stomach was left full of food without being able to empty it into the intestine, but with the surgery all the tissue that was obstructing had been removed, leaving the passage completely open according to its natural anatomy.

Coming out of the operating room and for the first two days, Caroline was very uncomfortable. As with any postoperative process, she was given pain medications and infection prevention drugs intravenously, as well as serum to keep her hydrated and provide nutrients. These first days were the most difficult, because they left her with a nasogastric tube (from the nose to the stomach), which drained the fluids from the stomach, to help the internal healing of the duodenum. The operated area had to be kept very clean to avoid infections; we could absolutely not give her any food.

Despite the fact that my daughter was always very brave, without crying or complaining much, these days she did have a very bad expression. Her little face reflected a lot of discomfort, pain and hunger. Despite this, she never asked for food.

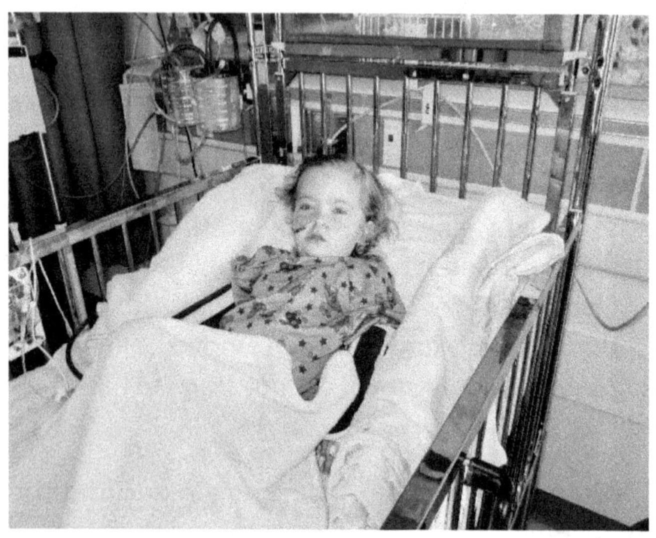

For me as a mother, they were also very difficult days, seeing her go through discomforts, but I was comforted by knowing that it had been for the good of her health.

As the days went by, everything became more bearable. Her general condition was improving, especially when the catheter was removed and we began to give her food, a reflection of relief was immediately noticed on her face, in addition to that, naturally the recovery of children is incredibly faster compared to that of an adult. Her stay in the hospital was difficult, it involved the process of recovery after an operation, but we were lucky that they allowed me to stay with her every day of hospitalization and even to sleep there.

They assigned us a fairly spacious room with a sofa that allowed me to have a good rest. In addition, being a children's hospital, they had a playroom for patients, as well as visits to the rooms of trained pets, to provide a restful stay and give the children a most pleasant distraction.

The operation was successful, the physical problem was completely corrected and we could immediately appreciate a decrease in the frequency of her vomiting, even though we had to continue giving her food through the gastric tube, since she couldn't accept food through her mouth because of the aversion to food that she had already developed from having vomited daily for these two years.

Once she recovered from her surgery, the gastroenterologist ordered another study, X-rays (Radiography) of the upper gastrointestinal (GI), in order to know how the digestive tract was functioning in real-time. An upper gastrointestinal (UGI) with small bowel series is an X-ray exam that shows the structure of the upper gastrointestinal tract, the part of the body that food passes through as it is digested, and the entire small intestine. The exam will allow the radiologist to assess how the upper gastrointestinal tract, which includes the esophagus, stomach, small intestine and small bowel, is working.[7] The study found her stomach functioning at 50% digestive rate compared to any other child her age. The doctor informed us that it was probably due to the anatomical blockage with which she was born, which had prevented this organ from working normally by emptying itself during the digestion process and that she hoped that with time, its blockage having been corrected, it would gradually begin to work normally.

Some weeks later, they gave us the results of the biopsies they had taken in that first endoscopy, and the diagnosis was an allergy called **eosinophilic esophagitis**, which has symptoms in children: difficulty feeding and swallowing (dysphagia), nausea, vomiting , abdominal pain, food stuck in the esophagus after swallowing, lack of response to medications for reflux disease, poor growth, malnutrition and weight loss; and if not treated promptly over the years, it can even cause a narrowing of the throat because the body, as a defense reaction, contracts. Fortunately this last symptom was not true in her case. Now, we finally had all the pieces of the puzzle together, and we knew the real causes of Caroline's ailments: the combination of the blockage in

[7] https://www.massgeneral.org/assets/MGH/pdf/children/pedi-upper-gi.pdf

her duodenum, with the terrible effects of these allergies.

Eosinophilic esophagitis is a chronic immune system disease that has identical symptoms to GERD, like trouble swallowing and chest pain. It happens when white blood cells, called eosinophils, build up in your esophagus, the tube that connects your mouth to your stomach.

These white blood cells are supposed to stay in your digestive tract. An allergic reaction usually makes the white blood cells move into the esophagus, which causes inflammation and discomfort[8].

The specialized clinic for these digestive disorders to which my daughter's case was referred, had been established within the same Children's Hospital in San Diego for only a few years. When they explained the symptoms, we realized that it was exactly what my daughter had suffered from birth.

There is no cure for EE. Treatments can manage your symptoms and prevent further damage. The two main types of treatments are medicines and diet.[9]

Until then, the only food that Caroline ingested was the complete nutrition formula, especially for children with use of a gastric tube, so we couldn't make

---

[8] https://www.webmd.com/digestive-disorders/what-is-eosinophilic-esophagitis#1

[9] https://medlineplus.gov/eosinophilicesophagitis.html

any changes in her diet, such as to discover or discard foods that could be allergic--like eggs, milk or nuts which are the main food allergens.

The treatment indicated by the specialist in the clinic was the use of oral steroids. My daughter was prescribed an inhaled medicine for asthma relief, which comes in a liquid form, and had to be mixed with ten packets of a sugar substitute as a conductor.

The aforementioned medication had to be given approximately half an hour before feeding her, so that it could work effectively. The purpose of mixing the medicine with the sugar substitute was to thicken it so that it could remain for a longer period as "smeared" on the internal tissue. This way, the effect it had was to cover the entire digestive tract with steroids, as a kind of protective layer until it reached the stomach, reducing the inflammation in the inner walls caused by the allergy.

I was really scared to death when I heard that I had to give my little daughter a sugar substitute! It is a no-calorie sweetener, obtained from a process that begins with sugar. Although this chemical called sucralose has the structure of sugar and tastes like sugar, it is not a natural product. I was quite concerned just thinking about giving this chemical to my daughter, not only because she was so small, but because of the large amounts she would have to consume. I had read about the harmful effects that these substances can cause in those who consume it, but finally, that was the appropriate treatment that existed at the time when my daughter was diagnosed, and what had to be done had to be done. I don't know if it's still the same treatment today. What I would recommend is checking with a doctor who specializes in this matter.

Giving her the medicine became a new challenge, because for the medicine to take effect, I had to give it orally and very, very slowly. This was precisely my daily struggle for the past two years before my daughter accepted food orally. Imagine now, what would I have to do to make her accept this mixture of medicine.

After a month of starting this treatment, my husband and I began to see much improvement in Caroline. The vomiting was very little, and over the weeks it disappeared, but she still didn't want to accept the food. However, my reasoning made me think that I should not continue to give such large amounts of sugar substitute to a small one--that was my way of thinking. My instincts as a mom again told me that there had to be other options to make the medicine work.

So I asked the doctors about what would be the second best option on how to give that medicine to my daughter, and they explained that in some cases this medicine had worked combining it with applesauce, which seemed more appropriate for my daughter, so I decided to mix the steroids this way. Thank goodness it worked perfectly.

On the other hand, the doctors informed us that, regarding the side effects that are commonly associated with the use of steroids, we did not have much to worry about. It was very unlikely that Caroline would suffer from them, because this type of medications passed very quickly through the body, without giving them a chance to be absorbed and enter the bloodstream. However, as Caroline was under this treatment for three years, in a preventive way she was undergoing annual eye exams to be sure that she would not develop glaucoma[10], which could be an aftermath. Another consequence of long-term steroid use that had to be ruled out was low bone density[11]. For this reason, studies were also done to check her bones, which came out well. However, when they checked her vitamin D level, which is necessary for the absorption of calcium, it came out low, and because of this, she had to take a supplement daily to reinforce the assimilation of this mineral.

---

[10] Glaucoma is a condition that damages your eye's optic nerve. It gets worse over time. It's often linked to a buildup of pressure inside your eye.

[11] A bone density test uses X-rays to measure how many grams of calcium and other bone minerals are packed into a segment of bone.

"Mother Nature will fall short of women by endowing us with physical endurance and muscular strength, but she amended the mess by providing us with two secret weapons: intelligence and intuition." -Joan Brady

With this surgery and steroid treatment, it would appear that the vomiting had been resolved. Now it was necessary to get my daughter to eat through her mouth, instead of through the gastrointestinal tract through which she was fed.

CHAPTER VIII

Acceptance and Adaptation

After taking Caroline to early stimulation classes in Tijuana, Mexico, which had served her enormously for her motor skills, it was time to look for some other option to continue helping her, since at two and a half years of age, she was in another stage of her development. Therefore, I decided to look for a school where they could accept her with the living conditions that she presented, such as receiving food through the gastric tube, but above all a place where they could participate actively in her process to overcome this situation.

I visited several private schools in Tijuana, but in the end I chose one that works under the Montessori system. I knew it was the right place for Caroline because I perceived several "signs" that could only come from God. Sometimes, if we are not alert, we miss these blessings sent from Him

First -This school had a ritual for lunchtime, making it extremely enjoyable, which was very important in helping to resolve Caroline's aversion to food.

Second - The principal of the school did not raise any objection regarding my daughter's gastric tube, accepting it in a very positive way. I had the reference of a previous visit to another school, in which the director requested a letter from the doctor responsible for the case, explaining Caroline's medical condition, as a way of legal protection for the institution. Just hearing this request, and the way it was asked, made me immediately remove it from my options.

Third - The teacher of the group to which Caroline would be assigned, in addition to being a certified Montessori guide, was also a nurse by profession. At that time I did not know her, but it should be added that later, once my daughter entered school and I got to know this guide, I discovered what an excellent person she is, and how well she received my daughter from the first day. She is the one who would be in charge of providing my daughter with her food during her stay at this Montessori School.

The food ritual was a process in which all the children participated. It included setting the table, sitting down to eat together, and giving thanks for the food. The menu consisted of a large variety of fresh and nutritious food, in a very beautiful environment. Participating in this ritual daily, and seeing all the children eat, was something that would be of great help to my daughter.

Part of the routine at school included taking a nap after eating, so while all the children went to sleep, the teacher took the opportunity to give Caroline her food, as she only observed the others eat during lunch, but was not eating anything, except for a few small tastes of food. She sat her in a reclining chair and thus with a little inclination she passed the food through the tube. Most of the time, Caroline would lull herself to exhaustion doing her school activities, and fall asleep after finishing her meal.

At that stage, we used an electronically actuated portable feeding pump, which automatically pushed the formula into the stomach. It was emptied into a special plastic bag that had a long flexible plastic tube, which was connected to the pump, and in turn reached my little girl's tummy. This little machine could even program the speed at which the food was given, specifying the number of milliliters that the pump would suck in during an hour. This feeding accessory was very useful, making the process much easier. The doctors did not provide it to me at the beginning, because they said that with this type of pump more artificial feeding became habitual and did not help the process of making her eat. Of course, this was when they thought that all Caroline had was reflux. Now I believe I would have experienced a lot less stress had I used this pump from the start. It really made a huge difference to use it, compared to the special syringe.

After a few weeks, the school principal suggested that it would be more convenient for me to pick up Caroline after the snack ritual, so that she could have her food by tube at home and could take her nap comfortably there. The usual class activities were mainly done in the morning, before lunch, anyway. The principal was right in considering it unnecessary for my daughter to sleep uncomfortably; I was very grateful to her for being mindful of my daughter's well-being, and for making sure that her time at school was always a pleasant experience.

As my little girl was already too old to eat in a high chair, it occurred to me to buy a recliner for children, so that she would sit there more comfortably in the time it took for the feeding pump to pass her food. First, I would always present her with different food options on the table to experiment with, and see if we were lucky. It was important to take advantage of the moments when she might feel hungry, with her stomach empty, and see if she could eat. Once we saw that she would not even try something anymore, we sat her in her chair, and gave her children's storybooks, coloring books, or sometimes we turned on the television with her favorite cartoons, to keep her entertained. Keeping a child of this age still is not easy, so we did our best to liven up that sitting period.

A few months after entering school, her teacher made the observation that she found a slight issue in Caroline's speech, and recommended that she take speech therapy.

Some time ago, when Caroline was 20 months old, in a routine medical visit, her pediatrician did a simple language evaluation, to check what level of development she had, and found that there was a bit of a lag, despite comparing it with her adjusted age. She referred me to a specialist to start speech therapy, since the number of words and phrases that my daughter used were very few compared to other children her age. As she was still very young, I preferred to give her more time to mature so that she could advance on her own in this area, in addition to the fact that these therapies would involve more trips to San Diego, trips that would add more fatigue to both her and me, so I decided to postpone this, giving priority to the other therapies that she already had on her schedule.

So when the teacher's recommendation came at Montessori School, I was not surprised. She suggested a therapist in my area, which was very convenient. This way, I would avoid more trips across the border, as well as having the advantage of being able to communicate easily in my own language with the therapist who assisted her. These sessions had a very positive effect on Caroline and were of great help improving her speech, because at almost three years of age, she was about to enter the first level of kindergarten, and it was very important to be able to communicate well with her classmates and to socialize. She took these therapies for three years.

I think it is very important and I strongly recommend to all moms, especially those of premature children, to be aware of the development of this aspect of their children's lives, so that as far as possible they are treated in a timely manner, since children with the slightest speech issue can become isolated, even when they can communicate and understand, but have difficulty speaking fluently. It can also affect their self-esteem, further aggravating the problem.

"Nothing happens by chance, deep down things have their secret plan, even if we don't understand it." - *Carlos Ruiz Zafón*

When it came to getting Caroline to eat through her mouth, we were still at a stalemate. This was another long stage that we lived through. Now we no longer had the stress of seeing her vomit every day, but we did live with the constant worry of when would she finally eat normally. Sometimes she would accept bites, little bites, but they were never significant enough to be considered a meal.

On the other hand, we kept going to occupational therapy, where they continued with the recommendation to expose her to food whenever she was hungry, and we continued to do so.

I listened and saw stories in doctors' offices of children reaching adolescence and still feeding through gastric tubes. I even saw a preadolescent young lady who had a gastric tube. It seemed inconceivable that my daughter could be like this, and in my mind that option did not exist. I was determined to continue fighting and looking for a way that Caroline would eat through her mouth in the near future.

Another experience during these years in visits to doctors' offices and hospitals was seeing so many children with various diseases and physical conditions that would be very difficult for any mother; for example, children bedridden in special wheelchairs, without any mobility, which made me realize how insignificant Caroline's difficulty really was. I was grateful to God that her problem was not a more serious one. Sometimes when we experience difficult trials in our lives, we believe that it is the worst thing that can happen to us, or that God has forgotten us, but just looking around is enough to make us grateful for what we have.

CHAPTER IX

When two dreams come together

My dream of being a mother would be completely fulfilled by having a couple of children, because I feel that it is a beautiful experience to grow up with brothers or sisters--those people with whom you will share the memories of your life. This is because I come from a family of four children, and I remember what a great gift it was to have their company, especially that of my older sister, Rosa Martha, the closest to my age. That was what I wanted my daughter to experience--to also have someone to share her childhood and life experiences.

Thus, along with times of uncertainty regarding my daughter, mainly due to not knowing when and how her eating would normalize, and feeling a great desire to see her completely healthy, I also had the great desire to have another child. On the other hand, I also felt a bit of pressure as I approached my 40s, so waiting for my daughter's complete recovery was not an alternative.

I asked God with all my might to help me make that wish come true. I prayed that he would grant me the opportunity to have a healthy baby, and I asked him to give me the strength to finish rearing my daughter.

There are people who do not believe in God, instead believing in some invisible force in the Universe; nevertheless; for me, faith in God was precisely what gave me the assurance that my great desire would come true. At that time I didn't know how the circumstances would take shape, but something I did know was that he would give me the means to mold my family as I had dreamed of.

When I shared these thoughts and wishes with Brian, he replied that in his mind, the idea of having another child was unthinkable under the circumstances in which we lived with our Caroline. My husband was primarily focused on the adversities that we were facing with her health, or on the very difficult problems that we had experienced as a couple, caused by the stress we were under. On the other hand, it was extremely sad for me to think about not being able to give our daughter a sibling, and denying ourselves the opportunity to experience a pregnancy and birth in more favorable circumstances.

Seeing my husband's reluctance to seek another pregnancy, I dared to make a risky decision. Without saying anything to him, I stopped taking the contraceptive pills, and after trying for several months to get pregnant without success, I looked for the same fertility doctor who'd helped me get pregnant with my baby girl. Perhaps he could help me conceive a baby again.

The doctor prescribed the same clomiphene citrate pills that he had given me the first time to stimulate ovulation, but after a few months of taking them unsuccessfully, he offered me another alternative. This time it was a stronger fertility treatment through an injection that promotes ovulation. I don't remember the name of the drug.

I remember almost like it was yesterday when the fertility doctor's office was about to inject me with this hormone treatment to induce ovulation. They warned me that there was a high risk of a multiple pregnancy. When I heard this, with almost everything ready to proceed, I had a moment of crisis in my head, a world of fearful thoughts came to my mind, imagining a multiple birth with the state of my womb, and at the same time the fear that I was doing it without the support of my husband. Within a minute I had to pause to consider whether or not to continue. But my great desire to have another baby was stronger. I took on the courage and with faith in my actions, I told the medical staff that I did accept the risks.

After a number of days, I bought a pregnancy test to see if I was pregnant. Since my husband didn't know about this fertility treatment, I had to do it outside the home. When I saw that the test read positive, I had a mixture of excitement and happiness, coupled with fear. How would I break this news to Brian. It was the only thing that made me uneasy. As to whether the baby would be healthy, I was optimistic and had no doubt that it would.

Maybe I could have come up with something really nice and creative to break the news to him in other circumstances, but when I remembered his attitude to the whole idea, it didn't inspire me to make the announcement in some “special” way. I thought about calling him on the phone. He was at his work when I did it, and the only thing that occurred to me to tell him was that I thought I was pregnant, because I had a delay in my period. As expected, he was very surprised at this possibility, as he knew very well that I was under contraceptive treatment. Without giving him more details, I only replied that I didn’t know more, but that I had the suspicion. I wanted to prepare him mentally, and give him confirmation of the news later.

A short time later, in March 2012, I was able to confirm with the doctor that I was pregnant. God gave me the opportunity to conceive another child, and I was happy! I always had the certainty that this would be the case, and that my dream of being a mother to another strong and healthy baby could happen. This news filled me with optimism, and I was equally confident and much more trusting that my daughter would make a full recovery.

To the contrary, when the news was reconfirmed, my husband was very fearful and uncertain. He felt that more worries and tensions would strain our family bond, and that it was impossible to successfully overcome so many difficulties with everything that we already were doing for Caroline, and on top of all this, subsequently add the care of a new pregnancy, and those of a newborn. He couldn't imagine how we would manage to survive this experience with well-being and peace. Besides, he was very afraid that this baby was also premature, and that we would have to relive the painful and distressing process that we had already gone through.

A couple of years later, I confessed to Brian what I had done to conceive Matthew. Either way, he always had the suspicion that it hadn't been a coincidence, but that I had sought that pregnancy. I know it wasn't the most honest thing to do to a spouse, but I couldn't think of another way to do it. I believed the reasons I had for having another baby were good for everyone--for Caroline, for my husband and for me, and that is what gave me peace of mind and a clear conscience, knowing in my heart why I had done it that way.

Brian's fear was not unfounded, since experience told us that my womb, even after corrective surgery, was not entirely suitable to hold the baby during the last months of pregnancy.

Despite my husband's extreme apprehension, there was a certain confidence in me that this time it would be different. I told him that he should have faith, that it would probably be a difficult time at first, but that it would be worth it. I believed that any problems would be temporary and that in the end we would have our two children with us, completely healthy and strong.

As soon as I confirmed my pregnancy, I consulted a doctor in perinatology, since these are obstetrician gynecologists with specialization in maternal-fetal medicine, and they are trained to attend pregnancies considered high risk, as was my case, or to attend deliveries whose circumstances are a bit unconventional. I knew that God would help me, but I also needed to use the best resources to be able to see my second child born without problems.

As in my daughter's pregnancy, the perinatologist asked me to perform the same tests to see if my baby was healthy and more now with my almost 40 years of age, but also in this case I refused to perform those tests. However, after insisting so many times, he asked me to at least take the blood test that did not put my pregnancy at risk, so I agreed to have that test done but with the same confidence as in my first pregnancy, that everything would be fine. I will never forget his words when he gave me the test results of the laboratory. The doctor told me that the numbers of the analysis were excellent, and he was somewhat surprised at how well they had turned out. I was very pleased but was not surprised, because I had all the faith that my son would be healthy.

It is important to remember that each case is different, and that is why us parents should always inform ourselves and investigate as patients, to put ourselves in the hands of the best medical professional possible. In my case, as I already had a history of bearing a premature baby, the specialist decided, as a preventive option for any membrane rupture, to do a **cerclage procedure**, which consists of closing the cervix by means of sutures or synthetic tape to reinforce it, helping to support the weight of the baby and prevent the cervix from opening before the end of the pregnancy.

This procedure was done to me close to my third month of pregnancy. It is a brief, minor surgery, in which they used general anesthesia. In spite of being a simple surgery, it was very painful afterwards. I stayed overnight in observation after the procedure, so that the doctors made sure there was no alteration to the baby, before they could let me go home that same day.

From then on, the doctor recommended rest. Even though I was able to carry out my daily activities, I had to be calm, taking care not to exert too much effort. So I tried not to walk a lot, or go up and down stairs more than necessary. I also tried not to stay on my feet for a long time, which was not always easy due to the doctor visits I had to do between therapies, gastroenterologist and Caroline's school, in addition to the routine check-ups with my gynecologist.

I have always thought that we must have an unshakable faith, but at the same time we have to do our part, and look actively for solutions to the challenges or problems that we face in order to see our dreams come true. I believe that trusting in God allows us to receive his guidance through inspiration, so that we choose the correct paths that will lead us to see our wishes come true.

Both the doctors of the clinic specializing in allergies, as well as the other doctors who periodically reviewed and evaluated Caroline, insisted that we continue with the occupational therapies, without really giving us any other alternative that would put us on the path to solving her difficulty eating. Despite having her health problems fixed, the years that had passed without eating orally, due to all the discomforts of nausea and vomiting that she'd lived through for so long had us stuck in the process.

Then one fine day, in a conversation in the gastroenterologist's office, the same one who diagnosed her correctly, after telling her that there was no progress she gave us another idea. She presented us with the option of an intensive program to help these types of severe cases with aversion to food. The doctor explained that my daughter would be a good candidate, and that there were very few places available, but if I was interested, she could enroll my daughter in this program. Immediately and almost without thinking, I told her that of course I agreed to let Caroline attend.

The doctor explained to me that to do so, Caroline had to enter the hospital together with me, where, among other measures, the food would be completely suspended through the gastric tube, to induce her more easily to taste food through her mouth. Naturally, my daughter would have medical monitoring 24 hours a day, since otherwise her health could be put at risk.

However, my pregnancy, which for obvious reasons had been diagnosed as high risk, was already advanced. In those days, I had already completed four months, so after careful consideration, I concluded that it would be very difficult to be able to stay in the hospital for two weeks under those conditions with Caroline, since this was the time that the program contemplated.

So after discussing it with the doctor, she understood perfectly and agreed with me that it would be better to wait, and agreed to postpone starting the process until after my son was born.

I was very excited to think about the success of this program, and I was confident that it would be the way Caroline would finally be able to eat naturally. I also continued to feel very optimistic about my pregnancy, and I had no doubt that my son would be born without any complications, so that I could spend the fifteen days accompanying her sister in this vitally important procedure. I saw it as another sign that God was granting me what I had asked for so earnestly. I was finally visualizing how and when my dreams would begin to come true.

God does not put dreams in our hearts, if he knows that they cannot be fulfilled.

About a month after seeing Caroline's gastroenterologist, and having completed five months of my pregnancy, I began to feel very strong contractions. I remember very well that afternoon. I was at home with Brian and my daughter when these pangs began, and although I was a little scared at first, it gave me peace of mind that this time and unlike my first pregnancy, I was ready, since they had already done the cerclage. I didn't hesitate to act fast, nor did I think about what to do, but almost instinctively I said to my husband: "I don't feel well; I'm going to the hospital." Unfortunately, it was not an option for him to take me, since it was necessary to arrive as soon as possible with my doctors, and considering that I had to cross the border, and that only I had the fast-crossing pass (a special 'frequent flyer' permit to use fast lines), I had to do it alone.

For some reason my memory didn't register the expression or response of my husband when I told him that I was leaving alone, but at that moment, we didn't know how risky the situation was, and I would not stay to find out either. My priority was to ensure that my pregnancy continued well, so with great determination I took the keys to my car, and left on my way to the hospital. Brian stayed home with Caroline.

On the way to the hospital, the only thing that I thought and asked God was that He'd allow me to arrive safely at my destination. As soon as I entered the reception to check in, I felt a huge relief and a great peace of mind to be there. Fortunately, they treated me immediately. After checking me, they told me that, thank God, my cervix was well closed, and that everything seemed to be in order. However, they did require hospitalization so I could be observed for a few days and they wished to control the contractions. Although I had to remain at rest, they did allow me to have a little more mobility compared to my previous pregnancy, in which I had to stay in bed constantly.

This time, I could sit most of the time; I could take a bath, walk slowly, and even go to the bathroom on my own. During those days I was hospitalized, they did some routine tests, and before allowing me to go home, they prescribed injections of the hormone progesterone, which I had to do periodically to help the uterus grow during pregnancy and prevent contractions from recurring.

The logistics of getting out of the house to have progesterone injections in a hospital near the house was not very practical, since our apartment was on the second floor, so it took me time to go up and down slowly and very carefully. All the appointments and activities with my daughter also grew complicated. I had to interrupt her therapies, both feeding and speech, for a few months and rely on my parents to send Caroline to school, because the schedules with my husband's work were not compatible. Brian and I had the enormous advantage that my parents were my neighbors, which made solving situations like this much easier.

Even with the injections, and having all the care, four weeks later the contractions started again, and consequently they had to admit me to the hospital for a week. I had to leave my daughter once again in the care of my parents, who took her to and from school, and took care of her until my husband came home from work.

While I was in the hospital for those days, I received the results of some routine blood tests that had been done weeks before, in which I was diagnosed with **gestational diabetes.**

At that time I didn't know what this disease was, but just hearing the word "diabetes" I reacted very badly. I was too concerned to find out about this condition, and I began to feel very physically unwell: I felt dizziness, vertigo, and severe nausea. I must have had a panic attack.

When the nurse came to the room to give me instructions and explain how I would have to take care of myself and control my sugar levels, I didn't want to or couldn't listen to her. I asked her to come back the next day, since I was very overwhelmed and had no head for more information. I needed to digest the news calmly. My mind was filled with negative thoughts, and I wondered now what I was going to do to fix everything that was happening? A daughter unable to eat, a high-risk pregnancy, and now managing gestational diabetes!

The next day, with a cooler head and a calmer heart, I could listen carefully to the nurse who explained to me how important it was, for both my baby and me, that I learn to keep blood sugar levels within the normal range. To achieve this, I had to monitor my diet by measuring my glucose after each meal, and writing down the levels in a log, to keep track. She also gave me a nutrition chart that contained different types of food such as fruits, vegetables, carbohydrates, meats, poultry, etc., with their respective calories per serving, to use as a guide in preparing my diet and complying with the suggested amount of food I should consume daily.

I was very attentive to all the information that was given to me, as well as the correct way to prick my finger to measure the level of glucose in the blood after each meal, just as diabetic patients do.

Gestational diabetes[12] is diabetes diagnosed for the first time during pregnancy (gestation). Like other types of diabetes, gestational diabetes affects how our cells use sugar (glucose). Gestational diabetes causes high blood sugar that can affect your pregnancy and your baby's health.

Gestational diabetes can affect the baby also if it is not controlled:

-The infant may be born very large and be harmed if it is born by natural childbirth;

-The child may experience rapid changes in blood levels after birth;

-It may be more likely for the child to be obese or overweight during childhood or adolescence.

---

[12] https://www.mayoclinic.org/diseases-conditions/gestational-diabetes/symptoms-causes/syc-20355339

Do whatever it takes

A few days later I was discharged. I was ready to go home and continue to rest there. I had some mobility as long as I did it calmly, remembering, of course, not to make any strenuous effort of any kind.

At home, I calmed down to plan my diet. In a short time, I knew almost automatically what amounts to eat of each food, avoiding the consumption of some that were very high in calories. This allowed me to maintain adequate glucose levels for the rest of the pregnancy, without the need to take medicine to control this condition. My priority was to take care of my health and that of my baby, always keeping in mind that the less medicine I took, the better it would be for my son.

Thus, the following two months continued, until around week 30, the contractions began to intensify, and although they were under control, I preferred to move back with my sister who lived in the United States, to be closer to the hospital in case of an emergency; which meant practically leaving my daughter in the full care of my husband and my parents. It was important that Caroline's routine was not affected, and thanks to the support of my parents, who were the ones who took her and brought her back from school, it was possible to achieve this. It was my parents who gave her meals through the gastric tube, while my husband came home from work to continue caring for our daughter each evening.

Meanwhile I stayed in bed most of the time. I only got up for the essentials, because I needed to focus all my energy on taking care of myself, to reach a successful pregnancy.

Definitely, without the valuable help of my parents, my husband, and my sister, who received me into her home, assisting me with the preparation of my meals while I was resting, and the intervention of several other people who helped me with the care of my daughter, it would have been impossible to take care of myself as I did.

CHAPTER X

The blessings begin

Around week 32, the contractions started even stronger, so I had to go to the hospital where they later admitted me, because in my condition, it was necessary to have medical supervision 24 hours a day.

This is how the last weeks of my pregnancy passed, trying to lengthen it as long as possible, trying to stop the contractions with different medications that they gave me in the hospital. One of them was magnesium, which was given to me intravenously, because it works as a muscle relaxant. It was expected that the uterus would respond in the same way by relaxing, and consequently the contractions would decrease. Unfortunately, this medicine gave me such a severe headache that I felt like I was going to explode. I do not know if other women have experienced the same, but I remember it as a horrible sensation, as if my head was in a very hot oven, I could bear it for only two or three days until I had to ask to have it removed, even though it did help me stop contractions.

On one occasion, I remember that I asked the perinatologist who attended me the reason why all this was happening again, if I already had surgery to correct the anatomical problem of my womb, in addition to also having the cerclage to strengthen the cervix. He replied that he was doing what could be done to maintain my pregnancy as long as possible, and that I had done the right thing by having rushed to the hospital to stop the contractions in time. In fact, the cervix was tightly closed, but it was my womb that was no longer supporting the growth of my baby. I perfectly remember his explanation regarding contractions, he told me how important it was to treat them and stop them quickly because they were somewhat like a car without brakes headed downhill, which, if it did not stop near the beginning, was much more difficult to stop when they were more advanced.

I spent several days practically alone in the hospital, since it was very far from my home on the other side of the border, and my husband had to continue taking care of my daughter and going to work. The days were bit complicated in terms of my emotions; although I was aware of why I could not be with my husband and my daughter, I could not help feeling alone. My younger sister was the one who visited me sometimes, since she lived closer to the hospital.

This time, when I was admitted, they placed a sensor strapped to a belt around my abdomen, to monitor the heartbeat of my son in my belly 24 hours a day. Everything had been stable until one day the baby's heart rate began to drop a lot. Suddenly, I remember seeing several nurses rush into my room. It was a very confusing moment, and I didn't understand what was happening. I just followed the instructions as soon as they gave them to me. They told me to lie face down, leaning on my knees and hands, in what they call a four-point position, in such a way that my abdomen was hanging in the air.

In a matter of seconds I began to understand better what was happening as I was feeling a lot of fear for my baby, because his heart was collapsing, so I just obeyed the orders, without questioning the nurses, until fortunately, his heart rate started recovering little by little.

From that day on, incidents like this started to happen more frequently. To some extent, I got used to the episodes without concern, because, thank God, I saw my baby recover when I took the right position.

As I approached the 35th week of pregnancy, my doctor, seeing that my baby was suffering from these events, informed me that I had two options: induce labor so that my child would be born now, or simply wait for the moment when they could no longer stop the contractions, and they had to take me to the operating room in a moment of emergency, to avoid putting my baby's health at risk, since every time the contractions occurred, he compressed and his heart rate decreased. In the second case, it would have to be a cesarean delivery due to emergency circumstances, where my baby no longer responded to the 4-point position that I had already used on several occasions.

In my mind the only objective was to reach the end of the pregnancy, so that my son was born without complications, and without the need for any medical assistance that would make him stay in the hospital longer, thus fulfilling another equally strong wish to give birth to my son, to be able to carry him and take him home with me. Possibly it is the dream of every mother who has gone through the experience of having premature children.

My husband and I asked to speak with a specialist in neonatology, to explain in detail the conditions that could be expected in a baby born at 35 weeks. His information was very encouraging, because according to statistics, our son had a good chance of being born healthy, so we decided on the induction of labor.

Two days before the scheduled induction date, the doctor requested that the sutures made on the cervix be removed to free the passage for the birth. It was clear that my uterus could no longer bear the burden of the baby. I can say that, by experience, this procedure was fundamental and beneficial to allow me to keep the baby almost full-term.

"Truly successful decision-making relies on a balance between deliberate and instinctive thinking." -Malcolm Gladwell

Another dream comes true

After my uterus was ready to dilate and give birth, the doctor gave me intravenously and little by little the medicine that would cause the contractions. I remember very well that they started at night. At first I didn't feel anything, but as the hours passed, I began to feel very strong pains throughout the night--contractions that came and went. As the next day dawned, now with ideal dilation, I was given epidural anesthesia and shortly after its application, my baby was born vaginally. I will never forget seeing my husband cry for the enormous joy of receiving our son without problems, who was checked, cleaned and placed on my chest. He was a small boy, about five pounds, but completely healthy and strong. When I saw my husband cry, it confirmed that I had done the right thing in getting pregnant without his consent. I was very happy for him too, that he received his son without any complications.

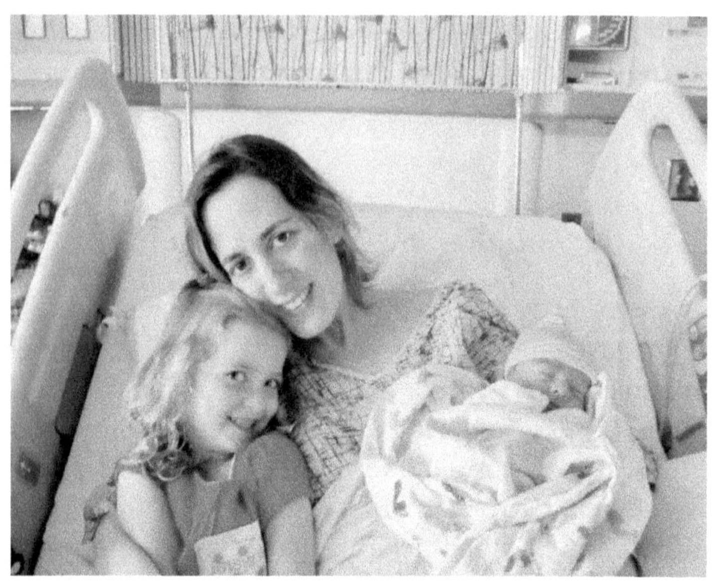

As soon as the baby was born, they checked my glucose level and the result was in the normal range. Fortunately, thank goodness, I no longer had any signs of diabetes, which was like "magic." They had explained to me that this type of diabetes is like that, it ends with the pregnancy, but seeing it as a fact resolved so instantly was a great relief for me. This was one more sign that we were going in the right direction with the help of God, to achieve very soon the other part of my great dream: that Caroline could eat through her mouth.

As a result of this gestational diabetes, I have been careful in my diet; all my life I have tried to nourish myself well, but after birthing my son I have done it even more. My gynecologist recommended that I be careful in my diet in terms of sugars, because the body can be left with some predisposition to developing diabetes in the years after pregnancy.

During the first days after Matthew's birth, we couldn't get him to drink from my breast, so again I had to use the breast pump to give him a bottle, from which he could not eat much. They asked me to write down in a log, the milliliters that he drank in each feeding, to be evaluating the progress of his milk consumption. If this continued, and the necessary amount of milk to be ingested was not regularized, he would have to be admitted to the intensive neonatal unit. While I would be discharged, since normally, after a natural delivery, without complications, the patient remains hospitalized for only two days.

However, we were blessed. Because the hospital was not full, they allowed me to stay in the same room where I had been staying, together with my son, until the fifth day. "Coincidence" or "luck"--for me it was one more blessing. I refused to re-live the experience of coming home without my baby, so I insisted with my son that he eat using a special bottle with a very small pacifier, until he accepted it and gradually increased the amount of food that he took, until finally he was able to consume the minimum necessary to be allowed to go home. My whole focus was on getting him to eat,

I was so determined to get him there that I allowed no other alternative.

Along with improving his diet, and before he was discharged, Matthew received phototherapy sessions in the same room for a couple of days. This is a very common treatment, which consists of exposing the newborn under bright lights of a lamp, to help break down the bilirubin that his still immature liver could not remove from the bloodstream.

This condition is called **jaundice**, and the doctor can easily diagnose it based on the appearance and color of the baby's skin, which turns yellow, as well as with a medical exam, blood test, or skin test with a device that measures the reflection of a special light that shines through the skin.

I later learned that this is very common in newborn babies before 38 weeks. Its detection and treatment is very important, since infant jaundice, although initially it seems a harmless condition, if not treated, can lead to deafness, cerebral palsy or other types of brain damage in the baby.

Fortunately, after being exposed to this light therapy, my child managed to demonstrate normal levels of bilirubin. It was a great blessing to be able to accompany him and take care of him in the room while he received these therapies.

Five days after birth, he was discharged. I dressed Matthew in a little yellow suit that my mother had bought for him especially for this moment, because, according to my mother's tradition, it is "good luck" for children to leave the hospital dressed in this color. I must confess that I am not superstitious, and for me the color of his clothes didn't really mean anything, but I put it on him following her custom, and especially because it was a gift that my mother had given my son with great love, to wear on that special day.

So we finally checked out of the hospital together. I felt immensely happy, complete, blessed to carry my son in my arms. Perhaps this is a fact that for most mothers is the most common and normal thing, but after what I experienced with Caroline, for me it was like living another miracle, because it meant that my son was healthy.

I always had the certainty within me that my second child would be born without any complications. I put all my faith into action, while researching which physician could assist me with expertise in perinatology.

I firmly believe that the first thing is God, the force of the Universe or the Supreme Being that many believe in, and then there is the action that each one of us exerts in order to see our dreams come true.

The love I feel for my children is just as immense for both of them, but that wound I had in my heart from the extreme suffering that I experienced at the birth and recovery process of my daughter, was healed after having lived through the birth of Matthew, by a normal delivery and having left the hospital with him in my arms.

My sister Elizabeth did us the favor of once again providing us lodging at her home in San Diego. As in the past, I wanted to be close to the hospital to feel safe. Perhaps this time I had nothing to be worried about, but the fear of the previous experience was real and latent. It was also practical, since we had an appointment with the family pediatrician to check up on my baby in a couple of weeks.

During these first weeks, I had to wake my child up to eat, since he could stay asleep all night without eating. I also had to move his feet or legs a little to rekindle his consciousness when he was eating. Otherwise, he would lull himself and begin to doze off shortly after starting his milk intake.

These types of behaviors, and other minor feeding difficulties, are expected in babies born before 34 to 37 weeks, because they have trouble coordinating sucking, breathing, and swallowing[13]. However, outside of those first few weeks, he was a

---

[13] https://medlineplus.gov/ency/article/007302.htm

baby with no eating problems, developing normally, like any other full-term baby.

Once Matthew was two months old, we made the necessary preparations and arrangements so that Caroline could participate in the program to treat her aversion to food, which months before we had decided to postpone because of my pregnancy. If you recall, both Caroline and I were required to stay in the hospital for two weeks.

My mother-in-law traveled to Tijuana to join my husband in the care of Matthew, and despite the fact that she was recovering from breast cancer treatment surgery, she was very happy to be with her second grandson; while her granddaughter tried to learn to eat properly. Therefore, we hired a nurse, to help my mother-in-law attend to Matthew with the night and early morning feedings, and allow her to sleep through the night.

During those weeks that I was with my daughter in the hospital, I extracted my milk so that I could continue to feed my son breast milk, just as I did with Caroline. Thanks to this wonderful invention of breast pump machines, it was possible to give the benefits of breast milk to my two children.

Having Faith will always help you find the paths that will lead you to solve or cope with any situation in your life.

Never lose it!

I always wondered why Matthew couldn't suck on my breast. At first, when he was a newborn, I thought it would be a matter of maturation, but when I saw a couple of months go by and I realized that he was not doing it no matter how much I insisted, I decided to settle for feeding by bottle. My whole focus was on Caroline's recovery.

CHAPTER XI

The impossible is possible

Leaving my two-month-old son in good hands, we started Caroline's oral food acceptance program. She was four years old by then, and it would not be an easy task. It consisted of completely cutting off the supply of food through the gastric tube, with the intention that when she felt hungry she would have the instinctive need to eat. This is why, initially, the foods that were offered would preferably be high-fat foods, since the amount that she'd begin to eat would be minimal.

The plan was to use the hospital room as if it were a hotel room for two weeks. Before we were admitted, I took the time to talk with Caroline, and I was able to explain in detail the program that would help her learn to eat, so that we could finally remove the tube that was in her stomach. Even though she was very young, I know that she did understand, because at no time did she cry or refuse to go, and the fact that I was sleeping with her gave her significant peace of mind and confidence in the process.

Finally settled in the hospital, we started the program. The gastric tube would still be inserted into Caroline's stomach, even when it was unused. We had the attention of an assigned therapist, who participated in at least one of Caroline's meals a day, and between the two of us we would choose and order the food that we thought Caroline might like, trying to provide food of different textures, but easy to swallow. The options were really a bit limited. We had to adapt to the cafeteria menu, since for reasons of hospital policy, food from another place could not be introduced.

When starting lunch, the therapist used techniques in which she invited her to eat as a game. She taught me how I must have a lot of patience, since something as normal and instinctive as eating is for anyone, for Caroline was something completely new. It came as a real challenge. We would sit down with her and begin to make comments and expressions like: "Hmm, how good this is, or that!" and immediately we would put the food into our mouths. Basically it was very similar to what we had been doing for years in occupational therapies, but this time we were doing it under much more favorable circumstances, stimulated by actual hunger and with the appropriate treatments.

Precisely because of hunger, on the second day of the program and after spending more than 24 hours without having received any food through the tube, she began to try bread and butter! It was quite an achievement to see how the food was introduced through the mouth. For example, she tried whole packets of butter, and she finished them in a few bites. The smooth, creamy consistency was probably easy for her to accept. It was like this, as she was trying bites of different foods, and even though not all of them ended up being to her liking, at least she showed openness to trying. This entire process was always under the supervision of the doctors, who monitored her vital signs and weight, in addition to keeping a log of her urine and number of daily bowel movements.

Something very positive is that the days that passed in the program were not traumatic for her at any time, in the sense that she cried or was uncomfortable when tasting the food. It was helpful that the nausea problem was controlled, thanks to the allergy treatment that she was still taking. At this stage, Caroline's difficulty eating was only a psychological aspect, a very strong aversion.

However, they were difficult days. There was a time when Caroline became very constipated, to the point of needing a nurse to assist her with the use of an enema, given that her diet was very poor in nutrients and fiber. In addition, she did not drink much water, no matter how much we insisted that she do so. But this seemed like the only way to take the big step.

The foods that she could tolerate most easily were those with a smooth and creamy texture, such as yogurt or butter. Those that required chewing were quite a challenge for her. At the end of those two weeks, there was a lot of progress, since my daughter was able to try and eat different types of food. It was definitely a great advance, a successful start of a process that still had a long way to go.

The first months after we left the hospital, I found myself needing to resort to the use of the gastric tube to complement Caroline's nutrition. The foods she began to eat were not complete foods. I fed her during the night using the automatic pump, which very slowly, almost overnight, introduced to her stomach the number of ounces equivalent to one intake. In this way she continued using the gastric tube, but in an unconscious way to her, since it was while she was sleeping. The purpose was to complete her nutrition, but without her awareness that she was still depending on the gastrostomy to be fed. This measure was one of the indications that the doctors gave me after finishing the program, to avoid any dehydration or imbalance in the nutrition, which could significantly affect the health of my daughter.

As I already mentioned, I was aware that this program was a good starter, but there was a long way to go. My daughter did not know any other way to eat besides the gastric tube, so she literally had to learn to chew to eat, something that we have all instinctively started to do. For her it would be a challenge that she would have to overcome, as she had psychological damage of aversion to food.

Many months passed like this, slowly evolving with the acceptance of more foods. There were several stages. In the first ones, she had at breakfast and dinner a very large amount of yogurt, while at meals the vegetable and chicken porridges were the best option, not because she could not chew, but because she did not want to do it because of the strong food phobia so rooted in her mind. Her tolerance for textured food was very limited.

But for me there was no turning back. After those first months of our stay in the hospital, I decided to cut completely her night feedings by the g tube and never use it again. I never lost faith. I never gave up and I was determined not to give her food again through the tube inserted into her stomach, despite the fact that there were days of great despair and frustration. I kept insisting--never giving up. In my mind that tube no longer existed, even though it was still physically there. That step had already been taken, and the only thing that had to result from all this was to get her to eat enough food to live and develop.

On many occasions, I lost patience trying to make her to eat. I admit that I was a bit harsh with her; I even remember that once my mother-in-law even told me not to insist any more. My husband contributed to a good balance in the dynamics of the meal, because just when I was exhausting my calm in the attempt, he intervened, managing to smooth the situation. Likewise, the lady who to date works at home with my mother, helped us by giving her porridges, which, although Caroline was already a big girl, she entertained with different activities that the lady came up with to distract Caroline while she ate. She would ask Caroline to help her cook or chop some food, while slipping the spoon into my girl's mouth. For me they were days off when she told me that Caroline had safely finished all her food.

As moms we can often lose patience trying to raise our children. Therefore, if possible, it can be very beneficial and even necessary, to have the support of a family member or someone else trustworthy, who is willing to help with renewed patience and tolerance, when one, like a mother, loses calm.

In this way time passed, and my daughter's menu was not expanding much. Watching Caroline consume the large portions of yogurt that she was eating for breakfast and dinner, it started to cause me some concern. Although the allergies that she presented were not to any specific food, much less to dairy, once again my instinct told me that so much of this type of food could not be healthy.

I had read some articles about milk and its derivatives and there was a lot of publicity on social media against them, even where it was mentioned that cow's milk was naturally to feed calves and not humans.

The truth is that the dairy industry has introduced us to milk as a vital food for the growth of children. For example, I grew up hearing that children had to drink milk every day to grow up healthy and have strong bones.

It may be a controversial topic, but some of these articles that I read made some sense to me, such as the idea that dairy could cause reflux. So, I decided to find some other food option that was easy for my daughter to eat and that was healthier and more nutritious at the same time.

"The intuitive mind is a sacred gift and the rational mind is a faithful servant. We have created a society that honors the servant and has forgotten the gift." - Albert Einstein

Again, while I tried to find better options for her and her health, things were presenting themselves in front of me in one way or another. I was struck by the trend toward vegan food and how it was becoming more and more popular. I think you have to be attentive to trends, as they indicate an opportunity for changes toward improvement. Right then, it turned out that two of my best friends were studying a nutrition technique called **trophology**, and after they told me about it, I decided to find out more about what it was and what its benefits were.

Food combining (also known as **trophology**) is a term for a nutritional approach that advocates specific combinations of foods as central to good health and weight loss (such as not mixing carbohydrate-rich foods and protein-rich foods in the same meal)[14].

I found it very interesting, so I asked my friends for a reference of the specialist with whom they were learning this new way of eating, and they recommended that I go to the nutritionist who had her office in Tijuana.

I had no intention of turning my family or my daughter into vegans, but I did feel that learning a little from this trend could help me to expand my repertoire of recipes, making them more nutritious, and trying to avoid dairy. The doctors never told me to do it, but something in me told me it could help us. Either way, I assumed that a more natural diet could benefit my daughter's health.

I got in touch with the nutritionist, made an appointment, and went to visit her. I told her about Caroline's history, and asked her to help me with an alternative to replace the yogurt that my daughter consumed in large quantities, something that had the

---

[14] https://dictionary.webmd.com/food-combining

similar consistency, but was natural, with good flavor and nutritious. She gave me a very good and very rich recipe for a fruit smoothie where I substitute the yogurt for **kefir** or also called Bulgarian yogurt. This is fermented milk rich in bacteria and probiotic yeasts, which improve the intestinal flora, help strengthen the immune system, and improve intestinal transit, helping to maintain the general health of the body.

The recipe for this smoothie consisted of mixing the kefir with fruits that were of the same type, according to the trophology technique, that is, sweet with sweet and sour with sour in the same smoothie. The recipe also contained seeds such as flax, chia, or hemp seeds, which are easy to incorporate into smoothies and provide plant protein. Finally, honey is added. This mixture, in addition to having a delicious flavor, has great nutritional value and is very easy to swallow, making it as thick or thin for my daughter as she would like. I explained to the nutritionist how difficult it was to introduce Caroline to new flavors, types and textures of food, and how limited her nutrient intake was, which is why she recommended kefir which, although it is also dairy, is more nutritious than yogurt and also has probiotics that help a lot with good digestion.

She suggested I make my own coconut or almond milk at home. As my daughter was accepting more new flavors, I began to include them in the smoothie, gradually reducing the kefir, until reaching the point where the smoothie had only coconut or almond milk. The amounts of these vary according to personal taste, the same with the amount of honey. They are added according to how liquidy or how sweet the smoothie is desired.

As for the amounts of seeds that are added, I was testing and seeing what texture it took with each one of them. Typically to an 8oz glass, I would add 1 to 1½ teaspoons. I tried all three seeds, but the texture varied a lot. With chia it became very gelatinous if it was not consumed quickly after making the mixture; with hemp seeds it had a very strong flavor; so the best option was with flaxseed, which is flavorless and does not yield as thick a texture as chia, especially when you buy the granulated seed. This recipe was very well accepted by my daughter, which made me very happy.

To date, my children take these smoothies very frequently in the morning. In fact, Caroline learned how to make them, and now she makes her own smoothie.

The eating habits with which I grew up at home were to eat balanced and natural nutritious foods, so it was very important to me to implement a similar diet for my children. I wanted to be able to offer unprocessed food, especially to Caroline. After having been consuming special formulas for so long, she was finally able to ingest natural and nutritious food orally.

We completely eliminated yogurt from her diet and from then on she began to accept more food variation. I do not know the scientific reason for this change, but what I can assure you is what I experienced with my daughter, when I changed her diet, and started with the seed smoothies, there was a very noticeable improvement, and she began accepting much more quantity and types of food.

I was so devoted to this process for my daughter as she was learning to eat, that even when we went on family vacations, when choosing hotels to stay in, we always looked for the options that would provide us greater comfort with small children, and certified that they had access to a kitchen or kitchenette so we could prepare the food that my daughter agreed to eat, and at the same time to give my son simpler and more nutritious food that sometimes you cannot find in a restaurant. Although it definitely involved more work for me to cook for them on vacation, it was worth it and it was preferable to continue watching their eating habits, but above all I was determined not to interrupt the progress with Caroline.

As soon as we got settled in on vacations, I went to buy the necessary ingredients to prepare their baby food, like those of any baby who begins to eat. I made them with chicken, vegetables, blended fruits, etc. On occasion, I had to ask for my blender to be replaced, as the one I had in my hotel room could not completely grind the chicken pieces. The transition which my daughter had begun–to eat through her mouth instead of through the gastric tube was still very recent, and my daughter continued to exhibit resistance and sensitivity to any minimal texture that she came to feel in her mouth, so during this period I needed to completely liquefy everything that I was preparing for her. But for some meals in the days during these holiday periods, I turned to yogurt again, because it was a break for me not to have to cook for her at least once per day. Plus it didn't stress me out making sure that she finished her food, since my daughter enjoyed eating every spoonful of the yogurt without any effort.

There were many occasions when Caroline refused to eat the porridge. I had to persuade her one way or another to do so. But I always had in my mind what the doctors said: "The more time passes, the more difficult the transition will be." So my approach was always to keep inducing her to eat through her mouth.

To be able to permanently remove the gastric tube, the doctors indicated that at least a year had to pass eating orally. It was more or less a reasonable time to let Caroline be exposed to illnesses such as colds and common infections of children her age, observing that her general health and immune system were not affected by a possible deficiency in her nutrition. Her diet should be varied and complete in calories and nutrients, to allow her to continue to grow optimally.

This was of vital importance, because if it was removed before the necessary time, we ran the risk of having to undergo another surgery to insert it again, in case her health required it. Naturally, my daughter got sick like any child her age, and as expected, when this happened, she lost her appetite and stopped eating a little. She even had several strong stomach infections with symptoms such as diarrhea, or colds with the classic discomforts, but I was always firm in trying to convince her to drink enough fluids through her mouth, without having to use the gastric tube, and to keep her hydrated, as this was crucial to her recovery. On some of these occasions, she lost weight, due to her loss of appetite, but it was also nothing extraordinary, she returned to her normal weight after getting better and regularizing her meals, as happens to any child of that age.

Thank God we never had the need to admit her to a hospital due to malnutrition or dehydration.

During that year the doctors weighed her, measured her height, and represented these measurements on the growth curves periodically, monitoring her development and evolution, in order to determine the right moment to permanently remove the gastric tube.

Throughout the years in which Caroline could not eat food orally, my husband lived in utter worry. It hurt him a lot to think that, when she entered elementary school, children could make hurtful comments to her for having the tube inserted in the stomach, and in this way hurting her self-esteem, which for me was not a cause for concern. I just wanted to see her free, without depending on that tube to feed herself. At some point I commented on this particular concern my husband had to the school's principal, and she replied that my daughter had already shown her little belly to her friends during a break in the schoolyard, and there was never any hurtful comment toward Caroline, they were just curious to know what it was.

It was a great challenge, the process was difficult and stressful, and I was determined to see her beat it. It was a daily, continuous task that required a lot of patience, discipline and perseverance. There were easy days, but other very difficult ones. However, I always refused to give in, I knew that only in that way would I be able to teach Caroline to eat. This phase of the porridge took a little more than two years, til she reached the point of eating food like any child of that age, without having to liquefy anything, chewing as anyone would.

Another dream, another blessing

Finally, at six years of age, the day came when the gastric tube was removed permanently from her abdomen. It was a procedure as simple as going to the surgeon's office one day, where they removed the "mickey button" and simply put some gauze to cover the hole. They explained to us that it would close naturally after two weeks, and that the skin would join itself without the need to suture it. One of the care instructions that the doctor gave me was that I should cover the hole with gauze when bathing my little girl, to prevent soapy water from entering her stomach, and he provided me with several special plastic pieces, patches with adherent material, which are glued to the skin to cover that area of the abdomen.

Another important recommendation was that I change the gauze for Caroline after eating, because since her stomach was literally open, the food she was taking could come out through the hole that was in the process of closing itself, and indeed it was, because it was necessary to change it after every meal. In my opinion, I would have preferred to put some stitches to close that hole in her abdomen, and in this way avoid the process of having gauzes full of gastric juices and food from the stomach. I felt that removing it and leaving it so exposed had not been the best way, but again I accepted and trusted what the doctors determined, because at the end of the day they are the experts.

Days passed, and I saw that the same amount of food kept coming out. There was not the slightest decrease in the spillage of waste; consequently, her skin was not joining as they explained it would happen, and therefore it was not closing the hole. Ultimately, the hole in her abdomen did not close during the period they predicted, so they had to intervene in a minor surgery, to close it with some stitches.

This last step has been one of the happiest moments of my life. Seeing that hole permanently closed without the tube that, although it had kept her alive for these years, was not a natural way of feeding or living. To my husband's relief and reassurance, Caroline entered first grade free of the gastric tube in her stomach.

God's guidance always accompanied us throughout this ordeal, giving me the intuition of a mother, and thanks to the fact that I always opposed Nissen fundoplication surgery; our rejection of it turned out to be a true lifesaver for my daughter. The doctors from the clinic specializing in allergies told me on one occasion that the decision not to have surgery on her had been decisive for the healing of my daughter, since if I had done so, it would have been terrible for the allergy condition that she suffered and undoubtedly also for the obstruction that she had in the duodenum.

In this way, thanks to God, we reached this long-awaited moment, after approximately three years of the aforementioned treatment of steroids for Caroline's allergies, years of occupational therapies, and annual endoscopies to follow her evolution, in which each time biopsies were taken to analyze the tissue and corroborate the functioning of the medicine. This procedure was continued every year, even after stopping the steroids. To perform these endoscopies, it was necessary to apply general anesthesia, with all the protocol that this entails from the hospital, which included a series of documents in which we accepted in writing the risks of this type of numbness, even if they were extremely low.

Despite the fact that these procedures were practically routine for us, there was a time when, in the middle of the paperwork to discharge her after recovering from anesthesia, the situation overwhelmed me so much that I suffered a very strong panic attack, to the extent that the medical staff had to help me, placing me on one of the stretchers. I had to call my mother and my sister to come and get us to return home--one of them driving my car, because I was not able even to drive. Over time I learned to trust God, and to have full faith in Him that these interventions would be carried out successfully every time.

Meanwhile my daughter continued to grow, overcoming all the obstacles that had arisen and that continued to arise.

The last endoscopy for monitoring occurred when she was nine years old, and this time she was discharged without the need to schedule any other follow-up study for the future. At this age, Caroline was already fully aware of the procedure, and although she was tired of going through general anesthesia once or twice a year for this study, she was always very brave, and I always accompanied her to the operating room where they applied the anesthesia, until she was completely unconscious. I explained to her that all this was for a good reason, and that we had to make sure that her body tissue was fine inside.

All these years really weren't easy for me or my family. We had our beautiful moments, as in any home, but faith in God and his guidance was what definitely sustained me throughout. He was the one that kept me going, even though I went through many moments of crying, despair, uncertainty and stress. Now that I look back, I realize that these were years completely dedicated to my daughter, since, although I used to go out with my husband or occasionally with friends, I did not feel good doing it. They were momentary distractions, because what I lived with my daughter every day, was still there in my mind constantly, always present. Always when I returned home after an outing, it was to face reality, one that caused me a lot of pain to see that my daughter was not completely healthy.

Dream big, ask with all your heart, it doesn't matter that you don't know how it will happen, have blind faith, and when inspiration comes, take action!

Today Caroline eats almost everything. I would dare say that she eats a much greater variety of foods than many children her age. She has also learned to distinguish what foods are nutritious, and she has a sense of what it is to eat healthy. Obviously, she loves sweets like any child her age, but she has enough discipline to know how to eat in a balanced and nutritious way. Still today, I am in awe when I watch her eat and enjoy everything from seafood, to meats, and even vegetables. The miracle that happened in her never ceases to amaze me, and I appreciate the path traveled. It makes me feel very proud and happy.

CHAPTER XII

The joy of the reward

Currently my daughter is 11 years old. She is a beautiful girl inside and out, creative and intelligent, and my son is a beautiful 8-year-old boy. Both of them are completely healthy. Our life is full of blessings, and every day of my life I thank God for my children. When I watch them play with their dad, when I hug them and they hug me, or when we kiss, I know it was worth all the effort. They are my best reward for so many difficult moments in life. Of course, like every mother, sometimes I lose my patience too, but, still, they are the greatest gift that life could give me. Surely all moms think that our children are the best in the world, and I am no exception. I don't think I could have had better children; they are two beautiful little human beings, for whom I strive to be a better person every day, and to give them a good example in life.

After having gone through years of therapies and doctors with poor diagnoses, I learned that we should not settle for the first information they gave us, especially if something did not make sense to us, and that we have to keep looking until we really feel convinced regarding the diagnosis as well as the treatment, so that they give us peace of mind both emotionally and rationally, avoiding the passage of so much valuable time wasted uselessly.

I have always wanted to use my experience to help all mothers of premature babies, especially those with children who require gastric tubes to feed themselves, or children who have severe reflux and who are going through difficult times. I longed to share my story and my experience. However, I did not know how to do it, until one day I took a personal development seminar. During on the sessions, I heard a speaker say that we all have a story to tell. It was at that moment that I connected that sleeping desire to help, with the "how" to do it, and the idea of writing this book came to my mind, narrating in detail the experience that I had to live and that, thank God, today I can share with a happy ending.

We all have an inner strength, which many times we do not even know is there, and it's not by accident or chance that we have it.

This force has been given to us by God, or by the Universe if you want to call it that, so that we learn to use it through our intellectual faculties, such as perception, will, reasoning, imagination, memory, and intuition. The combination of all these great tools will help us to get ahead of any situation that comes our way in life. If you have not heard about these abilities, I recommend you look for an audio or personal development book, since there are great teachers in this field. What are a few examples of the use of these abilities in my case? I had to use my will, which triggered the focus of concentrating on how I could get my daughter healthy and normal; reasoning, when I began to observe my daughter's symptoms; perception, in the way I saw my situation as small compared to other cases much more acute than mine; the imagination, which made me see and feel the future as it would be with my two healthy children; and the one that helped me the most, intuition, to receive God's guidance and reject that surgery to end the supposed "reflux."

My original intention was only to support the mothers of sick children, but by writing and connecting all the events that I lived through during these years, and to see how I managed to overcome each challenge, while strengthening my character and my mind with a positive attitude, I realized that these are the same components that lead anyone to achieve their dreams or overcome great challenges, to successfully achieve something that seems to be too big. This incorporates factors such as desire, faith, intuition, determination, perseverance and focus.

So, I concluded that maybe I could help by sharing my story with anyone who is going through difficult times in their life, and who needs encouragement and inspiration.

Another thing that I discovered when reliving my story by writing was that at some point, despite having managed to get a correct diagnosis, a successful corrective operation, and making certain my daughter was receiving the appropriate treatments, I felt stagnant seeing that my daughter did not progress in the food intake by mouth. But suddenly a new desire came, as strong and burning as that of being a mother for the first time: the enormous illusion of having another child. Strangely, it was precisely this longing that gave me new momentum to find the ultimate way to bring my daughter to complete healing. It's funny how things happen, but I think the desire to give Caroline a brother was the trigger for finding the right help.

I chose Faith as the title, since this is the belief in God, or the living Supreme Force, that guides us to achieve what we want so much. It is the strength of our inner self that leads us to feel our dream is alive.

This virtue applies to any deep desire that we have and feel from our hearts, and that is why I focus so much on it.

"Faith is the ability to see the invisible and believe in the incredible and that is what enables believers to receive what the masses think is impossible." -Clarence Smithison

As I was writing my story, I also remembered some episodes in my life when I held on to some desire and now, I know that those desires have to be strong enough to set our mind to work, focusing on what our heart really wants.

In my life I have experienced the great benefits of applying the concepts and recommendations that I've learned through reading, audios and attending seminars on personal development. I have noticed improvements in all aspects of my life, which gives me the certainty that indeed everything begins in the mind. This way of improving our lives really works, and I heartily share it with you. What I can tell you is that if you are going through a difficult situation in your life, never stop looking for solutions, don't give up looking for options, don't stop following your intuition--that internal voice we have that tells us there is something else, that you can always find other ways, and that above all you should never lose faith. This is the only thing that keeps us standing and enables us to move forward, in our walk through life.

When we are completely sure that our dream will come true, God shows us the path to take.

-Adriana Tapia.

LAST WORDS

Throughout my life I have gone through many stages in which I have desired to fulfill different goals or dreams, and during that process, I have learned that there is a watershed in my experience. This was triggered when I understood the concept of "awakening consciousness." That is, to listen to the deepest messages of our being, what we constantly speak to ourselves. I also came to understand how important it is to educate ourselves to identify and choose only thoughts of faith and not fear, always focusing on what we do want, and leaving out of our minds and our lives what we do not want within them.

From a very young age, I set goals and went after them. The ones I wanted most strongly were the ones I managed to achieve: finishing a degree, studying outside my city, finding my life partner, getting married in the place we dream of as a couple, surrounded by the people we love, etc.

Then came the unexpected–to be able to form the family, life and health situations that were not under my control; but thanks to God I managed to overcome, letting my faith comfort my pain, accepting that everything is allowed for some reason, and trusting that God's plan is always good.

In the same way I persisted in my faith--to raise my children and build a healthy and happy family. However, since I began to study personal development, and began to apply what I have learned in books, seminars, and courses, I have been able to solve situations in a better way, but always with faith as the primary element.

Learning to live in a constant state of faith is not an easy task, especially when we have great trials to overcome; but once we manage to do it, we can live with the best attitude to overcome the obstacles that appear to us along our way. And in this way, we are able to live fully.

"We all have an unsuspected reserve of strength inside, which arises when life puts us to the test." -Isabel Allende

www.ingramcontent.com/pod-product-compliance
Lightning Source LLC
LaVergne TN
LVHW050647100826
845148LV00011B/2015

* 9 7 8 1 7 3 6 4 8 4 9 0 6 *